INVENTIONS
AND DISCOVERIES
by Brian Williams

WARWICK PRESS

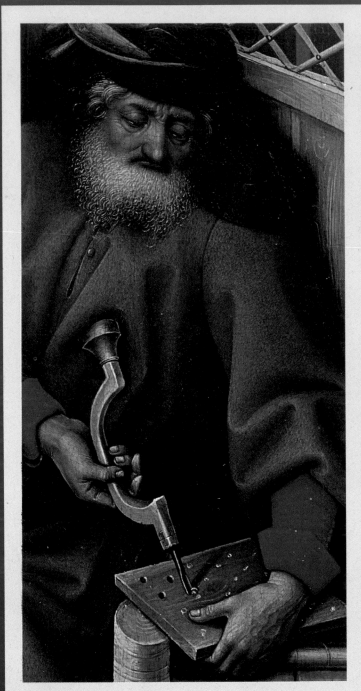

Previous page: A pattern of laser light. Above: A painting (c. 1430) showing a carpenter using a brace.

Top: A dish antenna. Above: An oxygen furnace in a steel works.

Published 1979 by Warwick Press Inc. 730 Fifth Avenue, New York 10019

First published in Great Britain by Franklin Watts Ltd. in 1978

Copyright © 1978 by Grisewood & Dempsey Ltd.

Printed by Vallardi Industrie Grafiche, Milan, Italy

All rights reserved 6 5 4 3 2 1

Library of Congress Catalog Card No. 78-63103
ISBN 0-531-09127-9
ISBN 0-531-09112-0 lib. bdg.

Author Brian Williams

Editorial Consultant Tony Osman

Editor Vanessa Clarke

Illustrators Nigel Chamberlain, Peter Gregory

Tony Gibbons, Eric Rowe

Contents

Chapter One THE FIRST DISCOVERIES   8
Stone Age Toolmakers   10
Invention for Survival   12

Chapter Two HAND TOOLS TO MACHINES   14
Using Fire and the Wheel   16
Metal Working and Early Craftsmen   18
The First Machines   20

Chapter Three ENERGY AND MACHINES   22
Wind, Water and Solar Power   24
Steam and the First Engines   26
New Fuels and Technology   28

Chapter Four THE STORY OF BUILDING   32
Tents to Skyscrapers   34
Builders at Work   36

Chapter Five INVENTIONS FOR THE HOME   40
Producing Food   42
Cooking and Canning   44
Lighting   45
Keeping Warm – Keeping Clean   46
Clothing   48
Entertainment   49

Chapter Six THE STORY OF MEDICINE   50
The First Healers   52
Medicine as a Science   54

Chapter Seven WHEELS, WINGS AND SAILS   56
On the Road   58
Traveling by Rail   62
Across the Oceans   64
In the Air   66

Chapter Eight WAR AND WEAPONS   68
Early Warriors   70
Gunpowder to Atom Bomb   72

Chapter Nine COMMUNICATIONS   74
The Story of Writing   76
Counting and Measuring   78
Books and Printing   80
Messages through the Air   82
Music and Sound Recording   84
The Picture Revolution   86

TIME CHART   88

FACT INDEX   90

Introduction

All discoveries and inventions spring from a question . . . why? Of all Earth's creatures only Man asks questions. Our natural curiosity makes us want to explore and examine the world around us. We use our eyes, our hands and our brains to investigate and experiment. And we remember what we learn, passing on knowledge from generation to generation.

Inventions and Discoveries traces the history of man the inventor, from the Stone Age to the Space Age. Some discoveries, as you will see, were made by accident, others came only after years of patient work and many failures. Key inventions often spark off a host of others. But an invention made before its time may remain unused, perhaps for hundreds of years.

Inventions succeed when people need them. The ancient peoples of Central America knew of the wheel. But since they had no domestic animals large enough to pull carts, they had no use for it. Similarly, when Marconi first demonstrated radio, the Italian government could see little purpose in his invention. Today we wonder how people ever managed without it. A man born in 1900 has seen amazing inventions – jet aircraft, television, computers, nuclear power, Moon landings – all marvels which would have been unbelievable to his grandfather. Such is the speed of invention in the modern world.

At the end of this book is a Fact Index and Time Chart. They tell you where to find information about a particular discovery, and also give additional information about inventions and inventors. For example, if you want to know when false teeth were invented, turn to the Fact Index. But if you want to read about progress in Medicine as a whole, turn to Chapter Six.

Chapter One

The First Discoveries

◀ A cave painting of a bison, found at Altamira in Spain.

▲ Grinding grain with a quern and rubbing stone to make gruel.

The first men lived together in groups. They helped each other in the search for food. They were weak and slow-moving compared to other animals so they relied on their brains to help them outwit their enemies.

With the apes, Man belongs to the primate group of mammals. All primates have hands. But no ape's hand is as sensitive as ours. Because the human thumb can touch any one of the fingers, our hands can grip objects firmly. But they are also capable of delicate movements.

When man began to walk erect, his hands were free to use and make tools. The first tool-using men lived more than two million years ago. They were meat-eaters, but they had no claws or sharp teeth like other hunters. So they picked up sticks, stones and the horns of dead animals to use as weapons.

To find a stone which makes a good weapon is a useful discovery. To shape a stone into a knife or a scraper is an invention. This was the next step. Man the tool-user became man the tool-maker. No other creature on Earth has managed this.

Man also has imagination. He learned how to observe his surroundings and make use of what he found. In this way he learned new skills. He learned how to make fire, how to tie knots and make nets, how to sew skins together to make clothes, how to tame wild animals and sow seeds. Now he needed a settled home. Instead of wandering from place to place, people began to live in caves and tents. The invention of pottery (about 9000 BC), metal tools (about 7000 BC), writing (before 3000 BC) and the wheel (before 3000 BC) were milestones marking the long road towards civilization. Man started along that road when he first began to use and make tools.

Stone Age Toolmakers

Man's first tools were the stones which lay around him. In fact long before true man, *Homo sapiens*, had evolved, primitive ape-like creatures such as *Australopithecus* were using sticks and stones as weapons. Scientists have found simple pebble tools over two million years old.

Near-men who lived between a million and 250,000 years ago were better tool-makers. They could shape stones into rough tools to use for chopping up meat and cracking bones.

Flint Tools

Early man often lived close to places where good tool-making stones could be found. The best stone was flint, which split into flakes when it was struck. By chipping away the edge of a flint a Stone Age tool-maker could shape it into a cutting or scraping tool.

The most useful of all early stone tools was the hand ax, which could also be used as a hammer, a trowel, a knife and a scraper.

Stone Age Cave-Dwellers

Early man lived in the open or in simple brushwood shelters. During the bitter cold of the Ice Age our Stone Age ancestors took shelter inside large caves. Here they were safe from wild animals. They knew how to make fire and had begun to cook their food instead of eating it raw.

The cave dwellers also needed clothes. They learned how to make bone needles and, using animal sinew as thread, they sewed skins together to make clothes and blankets. Ornaments carved with flint tools have been found in graves.

Flint-tipped arrows and spears made man a more successful hunter. Stone Age men hunted in groups and killed large animals, such as reindeer, bison and mammoths. All the members of the tribe, young and old, shared in the everyday tasks. This cooperation was an important advance towards civilization.

Stone Age tool-makers. The skins of the animals which the hunters killed were scraped and dried. They were then sewn together with bone needles to make clothes, or hung up to make tent-like shelters inside the cave. Axes, knives and spear-heads were made by chipping flakes from rocks.

Invention for Survival

Primitive man had to invent. He competed for food with powerful hunters such as wolves and lions. It was a dangerous world. He needed weapons, especially throwing weapons such as the bolas and the spear. By using his greater intelligence, he could trap large animals in pits and snares. And when he learned to make fire, about 500,000 years ago, man gained even greater power.

Neanderthal and Cro-Magnon Man

An early form of *Homo sapiens*, called Neanderthal man, evolved some 150,000 years ago. About 40,000 years ago the Neanderthals were replaced by a more advanced people. These were the Cro-Magnons, the ancestors of modern man. Cro-Magnon man had a brain much like ours.

When the Ice Age ended some 10,000 years ago, people stopped living in caves and began living in villages of tents or huts. Lakeside dwellers raised their huts on stilts above the water. They made dugout canoes and discovered how to twist plant fibers into rope to make fishing nets. They caught fish in basket traps woven from reeds, and carved fish hooks and needles from bone and ivory. A new weapon, the bow and arrow, was invented and wolf cubs, the first domestic dogs, were tamed to help in the hunt.

The Dawn of Civilization

Finding food took up most of early man's time. But in areas where food was plentiful, people began to stay in one place all year round. Several inventions were probably made by women, while the men were away hunting. They made pottery, coiling "ropes" of wet clay into shape and drying the pot in the sun or beside the fire.

The skill of growing food may have been discovered by accident, perhaps when plants thrown out on a rubbish heap grew again the following year. Soon seeds were planted deliberately and people began to tame wild hogs, goats, sheep and cattle by rearing young animals.

Civilization began in the warm river valleys of Mesopotamia. Here, where the land was fertile, men first became farmers. Tool-makers became craftsmen. And after 3000 BC, when the wheel and the first forms of writing came into use, the pace of discovery grew faster and faster.

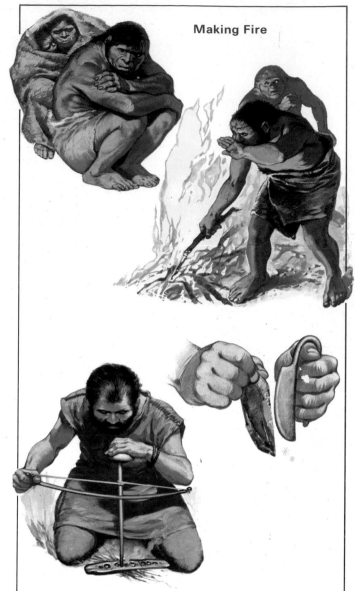

Making Fire

Like other animals, primitive man must at first have feared fire and fled from it. With no fur or hair to keep out the winter cold, men wrapped themselves in animal skins for warmth. Then someone, bolder than the rest, picked up a burning branch from a natural forest fire. He found that he could use and control fire. Once he had lit a fire, he kept it burning constantly. If it went out, he stole fire from his neighbor.

Later man discovered that fire could be made by rubbing two sticks together. Then he found he could strike sparks from flints. Fire was made in much the same way by striking steel against a flint in a tinder box right up until the invention of matches in the 1800s. A useful invention was the bowdrill, an Egyptian tool used at first in carpentry. This was a small bow with a cord twisted around a pointed stick. As the bow moved backwards and forwards, the rope twirled the pointed stick. The friction eventually made the wood so hot that it could set fire to dry moss and grass. When a series of Ice Ages came to northern Europe, starting about 300,000 years ago, fire-making became a vital skill. Without fire, the Stone Age cave-dweller could not have survived.

▶ *Japanese fishermen with a dip net. Stone Age lake dwellers made nets with a regular pattern of knots. The ability to tie secure knots was an important building and tool-making skill. The first fishermen trapped fish in shallow water while the Egyptians used nets to catch wild ducks and geese as well as fish.*

The Wheel

The wheel was probably invented in several places at about the same time. It was certainly in use in the Middle East around 3000 BC. Wheels may have been used to make pottery before anyone thought of using them to make transport easier. The use of the wheel led to increased trade between villages and towns. The traders took new ideas and products with them and in this way civilization spread and grew.

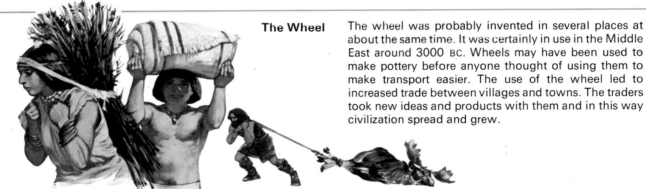

Before the wheel, heavy loads had to be carried or dragged. Putting wooden rollers beneath a load reduced the friction. This was a step towards inventing the wheel.

The first wheels were made either from sections of tree trunk or from three planks clamped together. Spoked wheels appeared around 2000 BC. The wheel also gave man a useful lifting device, the pulley, invented around 800 BC.

Chapter Two

Hand Tools to Machines

◄ *A carpenter and his tools from a painting by Robert Campin (c. 1430).*

▲ *A Sumerian potter, turning and shaping the clay on a wheel.*

Even in the Stone Age some people must have been better than others at making tools. Probably they were more curious and inventive than others too.

It was almost certainly one of these early "experts" who first discovered how to make metal tools. Perhaps he found a lump of natural copper and tried hammering it. Copper is soft and easily shaped, especially when heated in the fire.

This chapter describes how man the tool-maker became a craftsman. He discovered new skills, invented simple devices to make life easier, and began to use the materials around him – wood, coal, sand, clay and iron ore.

Metal-working was an almost magical secret. Metal weapons (made first of bronze, later of iron) were so much better than stone

weapons that people everywhere wanted them. This led to increased trade.

The smith, the "master of metals", became an important person. Other craftsmen also appeared, such as the weaver, the stone mason, the potter, the glass-blower and the carpenter. Many of the tools they used looked much like those you would find in a modern handyman's tool box.

With better tools, man could make better household goods and better houses to live in. To help him, he also devised the first simple machines. Some of these devices (such as the screw press, the lever and the winch, for example) have remained almost unchanged ever since. With his new skills, man the craftsman was on the way to becoming man the machine-builder.

Using Fire and the Wheel

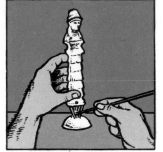

Casting by the lost wax method. A model was made in wax, then covered in wet clay. The clay was heated and the melted wax ran out

through a drain hole. Molten metal was then poured into the mold. When the metal had cooled, the clay case was broken off.

▼ The invention of the spinning wheel allowed the spinner to twist the yarn and wind it onto a spool at the same time. The medieval frame loom had foot pedals to open the "shed" – the alternate warp threads – so that the shuttle could be passed through.

The pedals worked a special frame called a heddle. Cloth was dyed by boiling it in vats containing animal and vegetable dyes.

Fire made possible the new crafts of the Age of Metals. It could change materials. It could turn wet clay into a watertight pot. It could turn sand and ashes into glass. It could be used to shape or mold metal.

Finding new uses for the wheel also helped man develop his new skills. With a potter's wheel, he could make better pots more quickly. With a simple lathe, he could "turn" a piece of wood to shape rollers and shafts accurately. Using a pulley, or a block and tackle, builders could raise heavy blocks of stone.

Metal Working

Lumps of pure metal, such as gold, silver and copper which are sometimes found in nature, were the first metals worked by man. The lumps were hammered into shape. Copper was the most useful metal for this purpose and by 4000 BC copper tools were being produced in the Near East. Sumerian metal-workers discovered that when copper and tin ores (the rock and earth containing the metals) are smelted together (heated to melting point) they make bronze. Since bronze melts more easily, it can also be cast into various shapes by means of molds.

The knowledge of metals was spread by trade.

▲ This Egyptian wall painting dating from about 1500 BC shows metal workers smelting bronze in a furnace. They worked bellows with their feet.

▶ The glassblower blows a bubble of glass at the end of a pipe into the size he wants. Using iron rods he can shape the glass or spin it into a flat disk.

▶ Greek coins. Most coins bore the head of the ruler on one side and on the other a state badge.

▼ Firing clay pots in a Mesopotamian kiln, around 5000 BC. The pots were stacked on a raised floor with holes in it, and a slow fire was lit underneath.

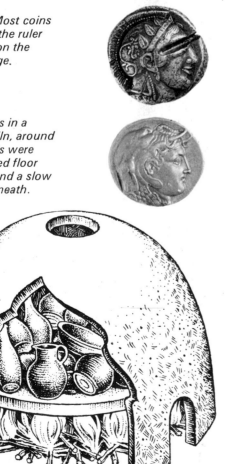

As trade grew, people needed a money system instead of the old method of barter (exchange of goods). The first metal coins, in gold and silver, were made around 800 BC. They were struck from a sheet of metal which had been hammered thin.

Pottery, Weaving and Dyeing

The potter's wheel was invented in Mesopotamia 5000 years ago. Early potters had many failures. Their pots either cracked in the fire or leaked. The invention of the kiln, in which pots and bricks could be fired slowly, solved this problem. By glazing their pots with a coating of copper or lead, potters made them stronger and more attractive.

Spinning thread, from wool or cotton fiber, was done by hand. The spindle, a wooden stick twirled to twist the thread, was the tool used until the invention of the spinning wheel in the 1300s. Weaving probably developed from basket-making, using spun thread instead of reeds. From about 4500 BC weavers made cloth on a loom, a frame which held the criss-cross pattern of threads. Cloth was colored with vegetable dyes made from plants, roots, berries and insects. This remained the method of dyeing cloth until the 1850s when a chemistry student, W. H. Perkin discovered a chemical dye by accident.

Metal Working and Early Craftsmen

Bronze continued to be man's most useful material until around 1000 BC. But earlier than this a new metal had been discovered in the middle East. This was iron, which after 1200 BC replaced bronze for most uses. Iron was far harder and stronger than bronze and so made better swords. To the ancient Greeks, iron was as precious as gold for this reason.

Iron was fairly common. The ore was first found lying on the surface but later, like copper and tin, it was mined underground. The ore was then smelted in a charcoal furnace. Charcoal was made by burning wood very slowly on a fire covered with turf to keep out the air.

The Iron Smith

In the late Middle Ages, blast furnaces came into use in which iron ore could be smelted at high temperatures and the metal poured into molds. Until then the furnaces produced iron which had to be worked again by the smiths. They did this by heating the metal again and again in their forges and hammering it. They used bellows to increase the heat of their forges. The smiths found that heating the iron slowly in charcoal and plunging it into water made it much harder. In fact, the iron was absorbing carbon from the charcoal and becoming steel. But, although the iron age smiths could make steel in this way, they did not really understand the process.

Smiths traveled about the countryside, making tools for farmers, miners, carpenters and stone-masons and weapons for soldiers. In this way metal-working spread from the middle East to India, and Europe.

Many of the tools used by the ancient Romans look familiar to us today. They include axes, knives, chisels, hammers, pincers, saws and sickles. Needles, pins, plowshares and fish-hooks were also made of iron. So were household goods such as caldrons and lamps.

Glass, Locks and Keys

Glass made from melting soda, lime and sand together was another useful early material. It was first used to glaze beads around 4000 BC and by 1350 BC there were factories in Egypt producing glass. Later, around 250 BC, Syrian glass-makers learned how to blow bubbles of hot glass on the end of blow pipes to make jugs and dishes of many shapes and sizes. The Romans brought this skill to Europe and glass is still blown today (see page 16). It was not until the 17th century that glass began to be cast and rolled into sheets.

As civilization developed and wealthy people began to fill their houses with possessions, locks and keys became necessary. Wooden locks were made in China and Egypt around 2000 BC and the Romans devised complicated metal locks with individual keys. The craftmanship needed for such delicate work was later turned to making other mechanisms, such as clocks.

◀ Chinese rope-makers. The frame they are using is an improvement on the primitive method of rolling plant fibers by hand. Here three sets of fibers are threaded through weights. As the frame is moved, the weights twirl around twisting the fibers together to form a rope.

CRAFTSMEN

◀ Chinese blacksmiths forging a sword. The blade is held on the anvil by pincers, and two sizes of hammer are being used. A less skilled workman, right, worked the bellows. The Chinese developed very efficient bellows and so were able to smelt iron far earlier than the rest of the world. In the 5th century BC they made cast iron caldrons and iron molds for the casting of spades, chisels and chariot parts.

▶ The Romans were great builders and stone was an important building material. Their stone masons cut and carved blocks of stone with many tools that are familiar to us today. Saws, mallets and chisels were used to cut and carve the stone, a compass and measuring stick to size it and a wooden pattern to check the shape. Only the bowdrill (center) has been replaced.

◀ Medieval carpenters secured wooden joints with dowels or pegs and glue made from boiled bones (left). The auger had replaced the bowdrill, and an all-purpose tool for shaping wood was the adz (center). Other tools had changed little since Roman times. The pole lathe (right) was worked by ''pumping'' the pole. The turner could hold his chisel with both hands for as long as the lathe kept spinning.

19

◄ *The medieval wheeled plow, drawn by oxen or horses or both as in this illustration, was much heavier than the hand plow of the ancient world.*

▼ *An Egyptian craftsman checking the weight of a gold bull's head on an equal arm balance. This kind of weighing machine has been used for around 7,000 years.*

The First Machines

Tools gave people extra muscles. With quite simple tools, the craftsmen of the ancient world were able to tackle such enormous tasks as the building of the Pyramids (see page 34). To help them they used tools which were actually simple machines. In a simple machine a small effort that moves a long distance causes a large force to be produced over a short distance. For example, pushing a heavy load up a ramp (an inclined plane) is easier than trying to lift it. The most important of these simple machines were the pulley, the wheel, the inclined plane, the screw, the lever and the wedge.

Useful Tools and Simple Machines

Many of the first tools were used by farmers. The plow – a form of lever – was an early key invention for farming. The first plowshares were hoes dragged by men. Later, plows were yoked to oxen and handles were added to the back so that the point of the plow could be driven deeper into the ground.

Watering crops in dry lands was a problem, so several devices were invented to raise water from a river or a well. Water from a well was drawn up in a bucket on a rope wound around a drum or wheel. This device is called a windlass. The "seesaw" Egyptian shaduf relied on the principle of the lever to raise water, while the Greek mathematician, Archimedes, thought up the idea

Men Before Their Time

In every age there have been geniuses whose ideas were ahead of their time. Democritus (born 460 BC) pioneered atomic theory with his belief that everything was made up of tiny indivisible elements. Later, Vitruvius, Philo, Hero and Ctesibius, Greeks living in Alexandria, Egypt, came up with a remarkable range of inventions. They designed pumps, flame-throwers, fire engines, windmills, mechanical crossbows, water clocks, surveying instruments and a steam turbine.

In the Middle Ages Roger Bacon, an English friar, dreamed of flying machines, mechanical ships, even cars. He discovered how to make gunpowder. But his ideas alarmed most people, who thought him a witch. Leonardo da Vinci (1452–1519) was not only a great artist and engineer. He was also a dreamer. He sketched plans for rolling mills, screw-cutting machines, tanks, a parachute and a helicopter.

Most people think that Albert Einstein (1879–1955) was ahead of his time. Even now scientists do not fully understand all his ideas. The dreams of inventors today will probably become reality in the 21st century.

◄ Mining in the 1500s. This woodcut shows an overshot waterwheel being used to drive a rag and chain pump. The wheel could also raise buckets of ore from inside the mine.

► Gear wheels were known to the ancient Greeks, and were vital to the working of machines. A gear system could change the direction of a force, so that a windmill turning up and over could work a grindstone turning round and round. These gear wheels are in a medieval windmill in Turkey.

of using a giant water-screw. Another Greek inventor, Ctesibius built both a suction pump and a force pump as early as 250 BC.

Using pumps, miners were able to reach deeper into the earth in search of metal. The ancient Romans used Archimedes's screw to drain mine shafts. They mined many metal ores and, in particular, lead which they used for roofing and plumbing.

Early builders used long branches as levers to lift heavy stones. Today the crowbar has replaced the branch but uses the same principle. Wedges were used in quarrying stone by the Greeks and they also adapted the screw in order to squeeze wine from grapes.

The Progress of Invention

Invention often means finding new use for an existing tool. The bow and arrow, for example, were adapted by Egyptian carpenters who used it to drill holes in wood. Later this bowdrill was used for making fire (see page 12). In the Middle Ages the bowdrill was replaced by carpenters with the bit and brace.

As situations change and people demand different products, tools and machines are developed and adapted. But almost all machines spring in some way from the first key discoveries about tools and the principles on which they work. When man learned to use other sources of power, apart from his own strength, he was able to make more powerful and more precise machine tools. Some of the processes described in this chapter are still carried out by hand today but in most cases machines have taken over.

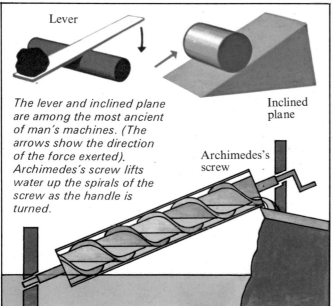

Lever

Inclined plane

Archimedes's screw

The lever and inclined plane are among the most ancient of man's machines. (The arrows show the direction of the force exerted). Archimedes's screw lifts water up the spirals of the screw as the handle is turned.

Chapter Three

Energy and Machines

◀ Testing electronic tubes before they leave the factory.

▲ This steam engine was built by James Watt in 1788.

Machines are devices which "convert" or change energy. For example, the steam engine changes heat into motion. Machines make work easier, because they are much more powerful than our own bodies.

When man learned how to build machines he could make the Earth's energy work for him. His first "power plants" were the natural forces of wind and water, and the strength of domestic animals. When he discovered how to harness these sources of energy, man was able to increase his power over nature.

Several basic simple machines have been used for thousands of years. But the machine age, as we know it today, did not begin until the 1700s and the Industrial Revolution. It began with the invention of the steam engine.

In this chapter you will see how the steam engine and the factory changed the face of the world and how man has turned to new fuels and new materials to feed his ever-hungry machines. Before the Industrial Revolution man used only natural materials, such as wood, iron and leather. Today we use many synthetic (man-made) materials, such as plastics.

Modern machines consume so much fuel that we need new sources of power – such as nuclear energy and power from the Sun. Because our machines are so complex, few inventions are now made by one man working alone. Michael Faraday, for instance, is often called "the father of electricity". But nuclear reactors and computers were built by teams of scientists working in cooperation.

Machines are all around us, at work and at home, as we move into the world of tomorrow – the world of electronics and robots.

Wind, Water and Solar Power

Early man lived close to nature. He knew the power of wind, water and sun. Without the sun he could not grow crops. But it took some time before he discovered how to make these natural forces work for him.

Wheels for Irrigation

Machines were needed when people began growing crops. In the dry Mediterranean lands farmers had to irrigate (water) their fields. Raising water in buckets from a ditch or well was hard, slow work even with the help of a pulley wheel or a pivot device, like the Egyptian shaduf.

It was probably a Greek who thought up the water-lifting wheel. If a number of buckets were fixed to the rim of a vertical wheel set up beside a stream, water could be raised simply by turning the wheel. The earliest power wheels were probably treadmills, worked by slaves walking inside the wheel itself. Animals could not be trained to do this. So a system of gears was invented. The vertical wheel was connected, through smaller toothed wheels or cogs, to a horizontal wheel. This horizontal wheel could be turned by an ox, camel or donkey plodding patiently round and round.

Watermills

Later someone noticed that the force of the water in a swift-flowing stream could push a wheel round on its own. This meant the process could be reversed. As the water turned the wheel, the same simple gear system could be used to make the horizontal wheel turn a grindstone and make flour. The Romans were the first to grind corn in this way. By the 1100s watermills were common in Europe and were being used to drive other machines such as trip-hammers and saws or bellows in foundries.

Windmills

The first windmills were probably made in the Middle East about AD 600. The sails looked rather like the blades of a lawnmower standing on end. As they turned in the wind, the wooden shaft to which the sails were fixed rotated and turned a grindstone.

Windmills with vertical arm-like sails first

◀ *A primitive windmill in Afghanistan. The twin sails turn in the horizontal plane, so no gear system is needed. The grindstone is simply attached to the lower end of the drive shaft. This was the first type of windmill to be invented.*

▶ *This is the world's largest solar furnace in the French Pyrenees. The curved, polished mirror focuses the Sun's rays to produce temperatures of around 3000°C. Flat mirrors in front of the large curved mirror reflect rays onto it as the sun changes direction.*

▼ *Simple machines which rely on animal power can still be seen working in the poorer parts of Africa and Asia. Buffalo are often used to turn a wheel to raise water from the local well.*

appeared in Europe in the 1100s. These wooden "post mills" were made so that they could turn and keep the sails facing into the wind. Inside was a simple gear (like the watermill's) which linked the sails to the grindstone below. In the 1300s the improved tower or "smock" mill was invented. It was made of stone, and only the top part or "cap", bearing the sails, turned into the wind.

Natural Power Today

Wind and water power are still used today. Some windmills and watermills still work in the same way but many have been linked to later inventions such as the turbine and the generator. Many windmills, for example, no longer operate one piece of machinery but drive generators which convert the energy of the wind into electricity. Electricity can also come from hydroelectric and tidal power stations.

It is also possible – even in cool countries – to heat a building by means of solar panels, which collect the heat of the Sun's rays. Using a natural source of fuel like this is becoming increasingly important as fuels for burning become scarce. So scientists are looking more and more for new ways of using man's oldest sources of energy.

Steam and the First Engines

The textile industry had seen the introduction of new machines in the 1700s and engineers soon devised means of powering them by steam. A system of belts and pulleys linked the engine with the power looms on the mill floor.

For a long time most goods were made by hand, usually in the worker's home and often by a family working together. But as new machines came into use, people began to work in factories. In the textile industry, Kay's flying shuttle (1733) made weaving much quicker and led to Hargreaves' invention of the spinning jenny (1764). Now spinners could keep up with the weavers. Next a spinning machine was made by Arkwright which was worked not by hand but by waterpower. The first factories were successful because they made good use of waterwheels, but it was steam power that really caused a change in the means of production and so in the lives of people in Europe and North America.

The First Steam Engines

James Watt is considered the father of the steam engine but he was not its inventor. The ancient Greeks had experimented with devices that used steam to create power and move wheels. But to them it remained a toy. In the 17th century von Guericke and Papin explored the possibilities of atmospheric pressure (the weight of air). They found that if you removed the air from below a piston in a cylinder, the air outside would force the piston into the cylinder. In early steam engines, steam was used to remove the air.

The first steam engines were pumps invented to tackle the problem of flooding in mines in the 1690s. Newcomen is said to have made the first steam engine in 1712. But it was not very efficient. James Watt saw its faults and started to build a better model. In 1761 he made an engine that could drive machinery. He did this by changing the "up and down" motion of the piston into a "round and round" motion, like the water wheel. At first Watt used a system of gears known as "sun and planet" gearing but later he and other engineers used the crankshaft, a device that had been in use since the Middle Ages.

Watt and his partner Boulton soon had a factory producing these engines. They were helped by the improvements in precision tools. Thiout's lathe (1750) and Wilkinson's boring mill (1774) were two of these machines that helped to make the parts of engines and other equipment used in the new factories.

The Factory Age

Watt's engines soon took over from the waterwheels in factories. They operated drilling, boring and milling machines and drove bellows for blast furnaces. They were used by other inventors like Cartwright who made the power loom (1785) for the textile factories and Nasmyth who developed the massive steam hammers which went to work in the foundries in 1839.

An industrial period began all over Europe and soon in the United States. In the 1800s people left the countryside for jobs in factories. More and more people became dependent on the wages they earned rather than the food they produced. Steamships and locomotives began a new age of fast travel. Crowded cities meant improvements in building; medical care became very urgent. As the engines improved, they demanded more and more fuel and raw materials. They gave scope to man's inventiveness in making new products and improving living conditions.

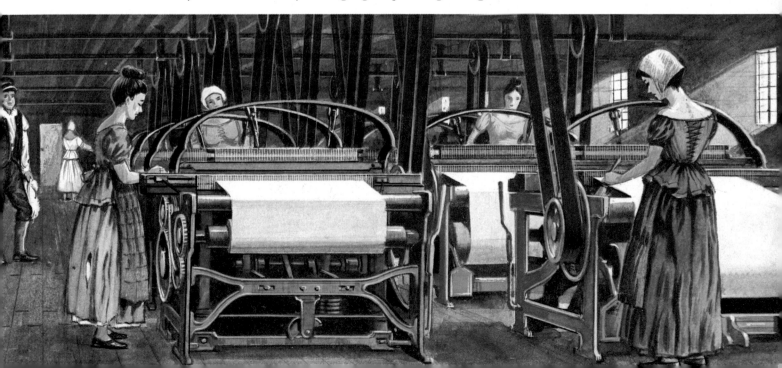

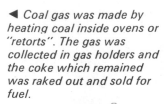

◄ Coal gas was made by heating coal inside ovens or "retorts". The gas was collected in gas holders and the coke which remained was raked out and sold for fuel.

New Fuels and Technology

Iron-making was a slow process, even after the invention of a primitive blast furnace in the 1300s. All ironwork was hammered or stamped by hand until water-driven rolling- and slitting-mills came into use in the 1500s.

In 1709 a Shropshire iron-master called Abraham Darby found a way of making cast iron using coke instead of charcoal (which had become scarce in England). Coke is made by heating coal to drive off the impurities. One useful by-product of coke-making was coal gas for lighting as Philippe Lebon demonstrated in the 1790s.

Coal was burned as a domestic fuel in ancient China and small mines were worked during the Middle Ages. Most coal was dug from outcrops near the surface. Deep mining was impossible before the invention of the steam pumping engine.

During the 1800s, as demand for coal increased enormously, new and deeper mines were dug. Around 1900 coal-cutting machines were introduced to make mining less difficult work.

Making Energy

Industry had powerful "muscles" in coal and water power. Water wheels were still used in factories in the 1820s, and water power became even more important with the invention of the turbine in 1824. From this was developed the steam turbine (1884), which is one of today's most important energy-converting devices.

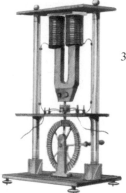

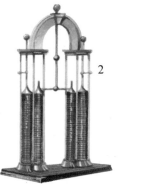

1. Faraday's disk dynamo used a horseshoe magnet and copper disk. 2. Volta's battery or "pile". 3. Pixii's 1832 generator had permanent magnets and armature windings.

Neither water power nor steam power could be sent from one place to another. Each factory had to have its own power source. "Long-distance" power and power in the home were only dreams until the development of electricity.

Electric Power

In 1752 Benjamin Franklin proved that lightning was in fact a giant electric spark by flying a kite with a metal key attached during a thunderstorm – a very dangerous experiment. He later made the first lightning conductor.

An Italian scientist called Luigi Galvani was skinning frogs on a zinc plate when he noticed that the frogs' legs twitched when touched by the knife. He thought the dead frogs contained electricity. But he was wrong. Alessandro Volta discovered that it was the two metals (the plate and the knife), linked by a moist "conductor" (frogs' legs), which were making an electric current. In 1800 he built the first electric battery – a "sandwich" of zinc and copper or silver plates between sheets of cloth moistened in salt water. It produced a steady electric current.

▼ *Benjamin Franklin carrying out a very dangerous experiment in 1752. By flying a kite during a thunderstorm, he obtained sparks from the end of the kite string which showed that lightning was an electrical discharge. This discovery led to the invention of the lightning conductor.*

▲ *A nuclear reactor under construction. In a reactor, heat is released by splitting atoms of uranium. This heat is used to produce steam which drives turbines and generators to make electricity.*
▶ *An oil rig on its way to an offshore drilling site. The modern world depends on oil, and new oil reserves are constantly being sought.*

Hans Christian Oersted showed that an electric current would move a magnetized compass needle. This discovery spurred Michael Faraday to make the first electric motor. By using a Volta battery to pass a current through a wire suspended over a magnet, he made the wire rotate. If electricity could produce motion, it could drive a machine.

In 1831 Faraday made the process work in reverse, and built the first dynamo. A copper disk rotating between the poles of a magnet produced a steady electric current. This simple device was improved by Hippolyte Pixii, whose generator was the forerunner of the modern dynamo. Faraday also invented the transformer, which alters the voltage (intensity) of an electric supply so that it can drive different kinds of electrical machinery.

Electricity, man's invisible servant, brought great changes, particularly in the home and in communications. By the early 1900s electricity was being used in homes, farms, shops, factories and offices.

Most of the generators which make our electricity are driven by water power, coal or oil. Oil

was first mined in large quantities in North America in the 1850s and was first used in oil lamps. It became a vital fuel with the invention of the internal combustion engine and the automobile (see page 59). Natural gas was discovered in the 1870s and is now another important fuel.

Nuclear Power

The newest source of power used by man is nuclear energy. The first controlled "chain reaction" which split atoms of uranium to release the enormous power locked inside, took place in 1942. This power can be used to make terrifying weapons, such as the atom bomb, or to drive generators to make electricity year after year, using only a relatively small piece of uranium as fuel.

New Materials for the Machine Age

In 1856 the Bessemer steel converter (which blew air through molten iron) made it possible to make steel cheaply and quickly. Huge milling machines, able to work metal at great heat, could turn out large steel girders and plates. This revolutionized the building industry (see page 38). Bessemer's process remained in use until modern times, but new more advanced ways of steel-making (such as the electric arc furnace) have replaced it.

To build new machines and shape new materials, man needed machine tools such as grinders, power lathes and borers. He needed to be able to make nails and screws and bolts in huge

▲ ◀ *The German alchemist Hennig Brand discovered phosphorus in 1669. Alchemists experimented with the impossible task of changing metal into gold. However they did provide a foundation for modern chemistry.*

▶ *A modern memory circuit containing over 120 components can be fitted on a silicon chip small enough to pass through the eye of an ordinary needle.*

▼ *These plastic objects from the 1930s are made from bakelite, a material invented by Baekeland in 1904.*

◄ A 19th century rubber factory. Many people experimented with making rubber goods. But it was not until after 1841 when Goodyear discovered a process for treating rubber, 'vulcanization', that products could be made that did not smell, crack or melt.

► Robot welders assembling cars on a Japanese production line. Computer-controlled machines can now carry out many routine tasks in a factory.

▼ In steel-making today, oxygen is injected into molten iron at high pressure. The refined steel is poured off by tilting the convertor.

numbers. He needed new materials, such as elastic (1820) and vulcanized (hardened) rubber (1844). An important new metal was aluminum, which was manufactured on a large scale after 1886. It was light, did not rust, and was a good conductor of heat and electricity.

Plastics

Plastics are part of our everyday lives. The story of plastics began with celluloid (1855), which was first used to make "imitation ivory" billiard balls and by 1888 to make photographic film. Other important plastics followed, including bakelite (1904), cellophane (1912), perspex (1930), nylon (1936), polystyrene (1930s) and PVC (1940s). Plastics are made from chemical by-products of coal and oil, combined with gas and molded at great heat and pressure.

Electronics and Automation

The computer (1946) and the transistor (1948) took man into the electronic age. Electronic "brains", which store and pass on information, can control modern transport and communications systems and run many factories.

In the 1920s "mass production" of goods became possible, after Henry Ford started to build cars quickly and cheaply on an "assembly line". Machines became more important than human workers. Today a factory can be run automatically, with robot workers taking man's place on the assembly line.

Chapter Four

The Story Of Building

◄ *Skyscrapers soar above the crowded streets of New York.*

▲ *This mobile crane has a system of pulleys to lift heavy loads.*

When man became a builder, he was no longer at the mercy of nature. By making a shelter to live and work in, he had begun to create his own environment. By building cities, roads, bridges, tunnels and dams man could actually change the landscape.

Every age leaves behind its buildings, or their ruins, as its monuments. The Egyptians hoped to defy time itself by burying their pharaohs in tombs beneath huge pyramids of stone. The Romans, more down-to-earth, left us bridges, roads, and aqueducts. The Middle Ages gave us great castles and cathedrals; the 1700s stately homes; the 1900s towering skyscrapers.

The story of building changes as new materials and construction techniques are introduced. Modern "factory-building" is far removed from the painstaking toil of the medieval stone-mason. This skillful craftsman may have spent his life working on a building which was not completed until long after his death. New materials such as reinforced concrete and steel, and inventions such as explosives and mechanical excavators, have revolutionized the way man builds.

Many of these changes happened during the Industrial Revolution, when factories and houses were built at great speed. Later, architects thought more carefully about "city planning". And today we try to make new buildings blend with their environment as much as possible.

Our homes are still shelters, even though they may be fitted with comforts such as air conditioning and central heating. Many of us spend much of our lives inside buildings – at home, at work or at play. The monuments of the modern world will not be temples or palaces but skyscraper office blocks.

Tents to Skyscrapers

When man was a hunter wandering from place to place in search of food, he built simple tents by draping animal skins over a framework of branches. Tents could be easily taken down and carried away when the tribe moved on.

The first farmers also built the first permanent homes. In the early civilizations of Mesopotamia and Egypt, builders discovered how to make bricks from mud and straw, shaped and then baked in the sun. Later bricks were fired in kilns.

The most magnificent buildings of the ancient world, however, were not brick houses but temples, palaces and tombs. Huge stone monuments were built in honor of gods and great leaders. To build the Pyramids, beginning around 2700 BC, the Egyptians had to be expert mathematicians and surveyors. Blocks of stone weighing as much as 1000 tonnes were moved only with the help of simple machines such as levers, rollers, sledges and inclined planes, and the muscle power of thousands of slaves.

The Greeks and Romans built for beauty and strength. The Romans used wooden scaffolding and lifted heavy loads with the aids of pulleys and

▲ The early North American Indians made tents from a framework of birch poles covered with strips of bark. A tent of this kind could also be covered with animal skins.

◄ Sumerian house-builders. Bricks were made with mud and straw and dried in the sun. Notice the woven basket and the yoke for carrying the bricks.

▶ The Egyptians had no lifting tackle. The huge blocks of stone needed to build the pyramids were hauled up ramps on sledges. Because they used no cement, the Egyptians shaped each stone with great care so that it fitted precisely. The set square and plumb line were essential tools for masons and surveyors.

cranes. Wood was then more plentiful in Europe and was used commonly in building. The Romans were also excellent engineers and town planners. They laid out streets and squares and piped water to their cities in lead pipes.

During the Middle Ages in Europe, the wooden houses of villages and towns were dwarfed by huge stone cathedrals, often the work of two or more generations of stonemasons, carpenters and laborers. These massive buildings needed secure foundations. Otherwise they were in danger of collapsing or leaning like the Leaning Tower of Pisa. French architects constructed outside "flying" buttresses to support the weight of cathedral walls. Engineers at this time, especially in Holland, began to improve canals and introduce locks and weirs.

Until the late 1880s few buildings were higher than three or four stories. This was because in order to support the weight of the upper floors, the walls on the ground level had to be very thick. With new materials, such as reinforced concrete and steel girders, taller buildings could be constructed without this problem. The invention of the safety elevator by Otis in 1854 made the skyscrapers of Chicago and New York possible. Within a few years, people in cities were learning to work and live many stories above the ground.

► Three inventions made the skyscraper possible:– steel girders, prestressed concrete and the safe hydraulic lift. No-one wanted such high buildings if it meant having to climb dozens of flights of stairs. The skyscraper's steel frame is embedded in massive concrete foundations. Ready-made concrete and glass sections are lifted into place by tall tower cranes.

► Medieval builders used cranes and wooden scaffolding much like those of Roman times. They had two useful machines: the winch and pulley for hoisting small loads, and the wheelbarrow. Wheelbarrows appeared for the first time in Europe about 1200 and have remained more or less unchanged ever since.

▼ The strength of the Roman aqueduct lay in its arch design. To hoist the stones into place, the Romans used treadmill-operated cranes.

Builders at Work

Early man built with the materials most readily available in his area – stones, branches, mud and turf. In Europe, poor people usually lived in wattle and daub huts. Wattle was a wickerwork of branches plastered over with a "daub" of wet mud. The same principle is used in a modern lath and plaster wall.

The ancient Egyptians used wall plaster made from gypsum rock, powdered and mixed with water. The wooden frame of a house was usually secured by wooden pegs, for until the 1800s metal nails had to be made by hand.

Arches and Columns

The high roofs of many ancient monuments were supported by tall columns. The Greeks built columns of marble or limestone and rested beams across them. The Romans also used columns and developed the arch – a curve of wedge-shaped stones joining the columns. The arch was a much stronger support and could be extended to form a vault. They also built domes, such as the Pantheon which rests on a wall of concrete, strengthened by a system of brick arches.

Bricks and Mortar

Ancient stone masons often cut blocks of stone so accurately that no mortar or cement was needed to hold them together. But the Romans invented a powerful "hydraulic" (water-based) cement made from lime and burned clay.

During the Middle Ages the secret of cement-making was lost. But in 1824 Joseph Aspdin rediscovered it. His Portland cement (so called because it was intended to look like Portland stone) is still used today.

Mechanical Muscles

Until the 1800s builders relied on manpower. During the great era of canal and railroad construction in the Industrial Revolution, much of the digging was done by gangs of laborers known as navigators ("navvies" for short).

To speed up the work, steam-driven shovels and steam rollers were introduced. And since the 1940s the bulldozer and other mechanical excavators have made earth-moving, ditch-digging and road-making a much speedier business, (for more about road-building see page 60).

▲ Columns and arches support the vaulted roof in this German crypt. Medieval builders took over these building techniques from the Romans.

▼ All bricks were made by hand until the invention of brick-making machines in the 1800s. Kiln-firing produced better bricks than sun-drying.

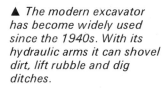

▲ The modern excavator has become widely used since the 1940s. With its hydraulic arms it can shovel dirt, lift rubble and dig ditches.

▶ The pneumatic drill was invented in the 1860s.

▼ The arrows show the direction of the load carried by each type of bridge.

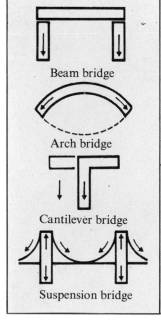

Beam bridge

Arch bridge

Cantilever bridge

Suspension bridge

▶ An engraving showing Chinese junks using an inclined plane, the earliest type of lock.

Bridge-Building

The first bridges were probably tree trunks laid across a narrow stream. The earliest bridges were made by hanging ropes or creepers from bank to bank, and fastening the ends to trees.

The Romans sank wooden piles into river beds and laid wooden beams across them. They also built fine stone and brick arch bridges and aqueducts. A few of these are still in use today.

Stone was the chief material for bridge-building until the Industrial Revolution. The first cast-iron bridge was built in 1779 and by the 1830s wrought

iron chains were being used in suspension bridges. Steel came to replace iron and the Forth Bridge (1890) was the first steel cantilever bridge. Shortly afterwards reinforced concrete came into general use.

▲ An Inca suspension bridge over the Rio Pampas in Peru.

▼ Elisha Otis demonstrating his safety lift in 1854. It was worked by hydraulic (water) power. Lifts with electric motors appeared in the 1890s.

Tunneling

Few long tunnels were attempted before the 1860s. M. I. Brunel invented a tunneling shield in order to drive a tunnel under the River Thames in 1843, and this shield was improved by J. H. Greathead in 1869.

The invention of dynamite by Nobel in 1866 gave the tunnel builders a powerful new explosive. The pneumatic drill, worked by compressed air, was invented in the 1860s by an engineer who wanted to be able to drill blasting holes in rock more quickly. Using these new techniques, the world's longest rail tunnel, the Simplon was finished in 1905.

Concrete and Steel

The Romans discovered that cement could be mixed with sand and gravel to make concrete. Concrete was used by them for walls and foundations. It is also an essential modern material. When wet it can be molded into useful shapes, which are immensely strong when dry. Concrete is used to make prefabricated (ready-made) buildings. The different parts are made in a factory, and assembled on the building site rather like the pieces of a giant jigsaw puzzle.

If thin steel rods are pushed into the concrete while it is still wet, it becomes even stronger. *Reinforced* concrete, as this is called, was invented in the 1890s. If the rods are stretched or *prestressed*, while the concrete is wet, it is stronger still.

Brick and wood are still common building materials. But we are quite used to seeing buildings made of metal, glass or even plastic. The first "modern" building with a framework of iron girders was built in 1851. A skyscraper's girders are its "bones", to which is added a "skin" of brick, concrete or glass.

The Modern City

As cities grew, they needed good water supplies and proper sewers. Poor hygiene caused disease, so builders had to tackle the task of providing towns and cities with water pipes, drains, pumping stations and sewage works.

Building engineers also put in street lighting and laid gas pipes, then, later, electricity cables and telephone wires. These vital unseen "arteries" keep a modern city alive.

Interior Decoration

Rich people have always wanted to decorate the inside of their homes. Wealthy Egyptians and Romans lived in great luxury. Their walls were decorated with painted scenes, and their floors were inlaid with glazed tiles and mosaic patterns. Carpets, woven by hand on a simple frame loom, were first made in ancient Egypt and Assyria, and the skill spread to Turkey, Persia, India and China.

Europe lagged behind until the end of the Middle Ages. Tapestries were hung on the cold stone walls of castles. Floors were bare or spread with rushes. It must have been very drafty, since few windows had glass until the 1500s. Glass was reserved for churches, and the art of stained glass reached a peak in the great cathedrals of the Middle Ages.

From the 1500s furniture-making developed steadily. Sideboards and bedsteads were prized possessions, and in the 1700s cabinet-makers such as Chippendale set new standards of elegance. By this time rugs were laid on the floor and walls were often paneled in wood. The first wallpaper, made by hand in small sheets, dates from around 1500. It became popular and in the 1800s, rolls of machine-made wallpaper appeared in the shops. Linoleum, a mixture of oxygen and linseed oil on a fabric base, was a hard-wearing and cheap floor covering invented in 1860.

Chapter Five

Inventions for the Home

◄ *Village life in the 1500s;*
from a painting by Pieter
Brueghel the Younger
(c. 1564–1637).

▲ *This 19th century*
American cooking range
enclosed the fire and had a
hot water boiler.

Domestic life began when man became a farmer and settled down to live in a permanent home. Farming provided him with a reliable food supply, as well as materials (such as cotton and wool) with which to clothe himself and make his home more comfortable.

The ancient civilizations of India and Rome set surprisingly high standards of comfort and hygiene. For example, the Romans had drains, piped water, baths and central heating in the houses of the rich and in public buildings. Such luxuries were unknown in medieval Europe, when home life was drafty, dirty, smoky and almost certainly smelly. They had to be re-invented in the 1800s.

Inside our homes we can create our own environment. We can make our own light, keep ourselves warm and clean, provide ourselves with clothing and furniture, and store and cook our food. Science played little part in home life until the 1700s when the Industrial Revolution began to change the way people lived – the clothes they wore, the food they ate, the entertainments they enjoyed, and the homes they lived in.

Many of the domestic inventions of the past 100 years are now so much part of our daily lives that we seldom stop to think about them – electric light, for instance. Since the 1800s advertising has done much to speed domestic invention, by encouraging people to buy new gadgets and to eat new "convenience" foods. Every year budding inventors with new ideas try to emulate the success of King C. Gillette, who invented the safety razor, and the Kellogg brothers who gave us breakfast cereals.

Producing Food

Farming began some time before 7000 BC, somewhere in the Middle East. Stone Age man discovered that instead of gathering plants, he could plant and grow them, and instead of hunting animals, he could keep herds of tame cattle, sheep, goats and pigs. It is likely that man harvested the wild grass-like ancestors of wheat and barley before (probably by accident) he learned to sow their seeds.

Farming in the Ancient World
The first farmers cleared the land by burning and scratched the surface with crude digging sticks. In the fertile valleys of Mesopotamia and Egypt, farmers used small hand plows and relied on the yearly river floods to enrich and water their land. To irrigate, or artificially water, their crops they had to invent machines to raise water and build canals, ditches and dams.

Seed was sown by hand and the corn cut with a flint (later bronze or iron) sickle. The grain was threshed by hand with a flail, or crushed beneath wooden rollers. The Romans practised a system of "rotation", resting the land by letting it lie fallow for a year between sowings. They were also beekeepers – honey was the most common sweetener in Europe until New World sugar became widely available after 1650.

Farming in Europe
The farmers of northern Europe developed a heavy ox-drawn plow, which cut and turned the soil into a furrow. Heavy plows needed very large fields, so farmers divided the land into strips and shared the work.

After the 1400s, rich farmers began to "enclose" their land with hedges. This made it possible to experiment with new crops. In the 1650s turnips and clover were introduced in England as winter feed. Before this most animals had to be killed in the fall, for there was no way of feeding them through the winter. Now larger, heavier animals could be bred.

Many modern vegetables were unknown in the Middle Ages or were grown in one region only. Potatoes and tomatoes were brought to Europe from the New World in the 1500s.

A farm in ancient Egypt. Irrigation water was raised into ditches by a shaduf. The farmers tilled the soil with mattocks and ox-drawn scratch plows. Grain was stored inside mud granaries and farm animals included geese, cattle, goats and donkeys. Fig trees and date palms were grown.

The Development of Farming

7000 BC	Beginnings of agriculture; the sowing of seed to grow grain and the rearing of domestic animals
4000 BC	Irrigation of crops in Mesopotamia and Egypt; use of hoes and sickles
500 BC	Iron tools in fairly general use; invention of the heavy plow drawn by yoked oxen
100 BC	Roman farmers rotate their crops
600 AD	Open-field system common in northern Europe with rotation of crops
1400s	Enclosure of open fields taking place; sheep-rearing very important
1500s	New plants brought from America to Europe
1650s	Clover and turnips provide winter fodder for animals
1700s	Scientific experimental farms improve growing methods; Tull's seed drill, 1701
1750s	Plantations and estates in the Americas growing tea, coffee, rubber, corn; Eli Whitney invents the cotton gin, 1793
1800s	Threshing and reaping machines; canning and refrigeration means many foodstuffs are now available all year round; steam power, 1840s; combine harvesters and new fertilizers; lawnmower 1832
1900s	Widespread use of chemical fertilizers, weedkillers and insecticides; miracle disease-resistant plants and factory farming

The Farming Revolution

Farming did not begin to change rapidly until the 1700s, when more food was urgently needed to feed a fast-growing population. New machines were invented to cope with this demand – Jethro Tull's seed drill (1701), Andrew Meikle's threshing machine (1784) and Cyrus McCormick's reaper (1834) and reaper-binder (1873).

The growth of science led to further improvements. After the 1750s men like Lavoisier and von Liebig established scientific principles for farming, such as the use of fertilizers and the alternation of root and grain crops. Experimental farms increased food production and introduced better methods of keeping and breeding animals.

Nitrogen based chemical fertilizers were first made just after 1900. In the 1940s chemical insecticides (such as DDT) and weed killers came into use. However, chemicals can harm both soil and wildlife. So scientists are trying to discover safer methods of killing pests. They also want to develop crops which can resist disease. Today in some parts of the world the use of scientific methods and machines means that only a few people are needed to work the land.

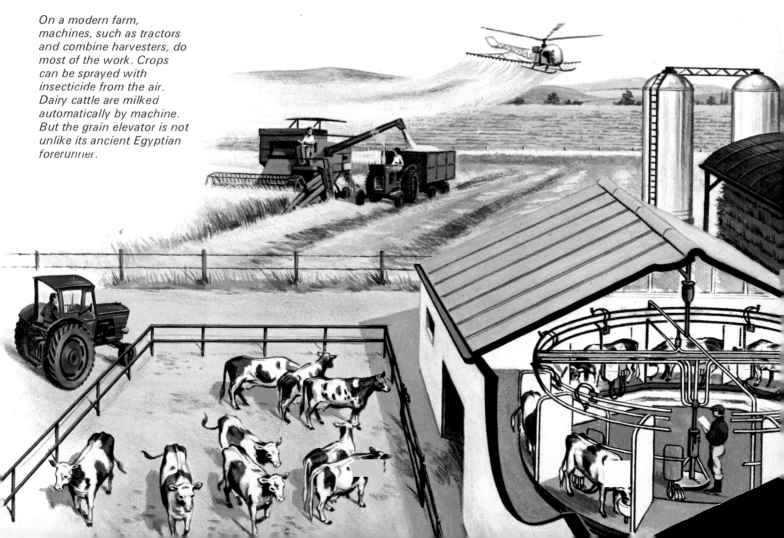

On a modern farm, machines, such as tractors and combine harvesters, do most of the work. Crops can be sprayed with insecticide from the air. Dairy cattle are milked automatically by machine. But the grain elevator is not unlike its ancient Egyptian forerunner.

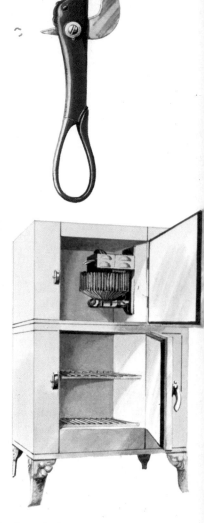

Cooking and Canning

Prehistoric man ate his meat raw. Cooking probably began by accident, when a joint of meat was left too near the fire, was burned, eaten and found to be tasty and tender. Stone Age cooks usually roasted their meat on spits or baked it on hot stones. As man's skills developed, cooking methods increased. Potters and smiths made pots and pans for boiling or baking food. Kilns and furnaces sparked off the idea for enclosed ovens. By the 1780s cast iron ranges that enclosed the open fire appeared, and a century later paraffin or gas cookers were in common use.

As women began to look for work outside the home, gadgets were invented to save time and labor – such as the electric toaster in the 1920s. Electric cookers became popular in the 1930s as public supplies of electric power became available.

Preserving Food

Early man discovered that meat and fish could be preserved by drying them in the sun. The Egyptians may have been the first to use salt to preserve food. The seamen who brought important new foods from America to Europe in the 16th century – such as the potato – lived on a diet of salt pork and dry biscuits.

Napoleon faced a similar problem in feeding his armies on long campaigns. He offered a prize for a ...tion. It was won by Nicolas Appert who in

▲ *A pork packing and canning factory in Chicago, 1880, used "everything but the grunt" of a pig.*

▶ *At first cans were opened with a hammer and chisel. The bull's head can opener (top) appeared in the 1860s.*

▶ *An Electrolux refrigerator of 1927. Refrigerators for the home came on the market in the late 1860s.*

1809 found that food boiled and then stored inside sealed jars would keep fresh. In the 1820s preserved food in metal cans went on sale for the first time. The reason why canned food keeps fresh, as Louis Pasteur discovered, is that heating the can kills the bacteria which caused decay. The first cans were opened with a hammer and chisel. The earliest can-opener was invented in the 1860s, but the inventor is unknown.

Freezing

Long before people had refrigerators, they stored winter ice inside special stone ice-houses. Since Roman times people had enjoyed eating ice cream and other cold dishes. In 1834, Jacob Perkins discovered a method of making ice artificially. By the 1870s refrigerators for home use were on sale and refrigerated ships were bringing frozen meat to Europe from Australia and America. Frozen foods were first sold in the 1920s. They changed people's eating habits almost as much as breakfast cereals, which appeared earlier, in the 1890s.

◄ *The pressure cooker was invented by Papin in 1679. This model dates from the 1930s.*

▼ *The microwave oven (1948) cooks very rapidly, by using radio waves to generate heat inside the food being cooked.*

▼ *Non-stick cooking pans were developed in the 1950s using the plastic PTFE.*

Lighting

As well as cooking his food, fire also gave early man light. The first lamps were blazing torches but early man also lit his cave with lamps made from hollowed stones filled with animal fat.

The oil lamp, like the candle, was one of the earliest and most useful inventions. Wicks were made first of reeds, then of linen. But oil lamps remained smoky and rather smelly until 1784 when Aimé Argand invented the tubular wick and a glass chimney to shield the flame from drafts. The discovery of huge reserves of paraffin (kerosene) in Pennsylvania in 1859 led to it replacing oil in lamps.

By the late 1700s experiments were being made with coal and gas lighting. In 1807 Pall Mall, London, had the first street gas lamps and soon many houses in Europe and America had gas lighting. Gas lamps were much improved in 1885 by the invention of the incandescent (glowing) mantle, a sleeve of cotton soaked in chemicals which fitted over the flame and spread the light.

Soon gas was challenged by a bright new rival – electricity. Joseph Swan (1878) and Thomas Edison (1879) each invented an electric filament lamp, an airless glass bulb containing a thread-like strip of carbon which glowed when a current passed through it.

Roman oil lamp

Candle

Lighting

The ancient Romans used clay oil lamps. A linen wick was soaked in the oil and held in a spout. Oil lamps were much improved by Aimé Argand's burner (1784). Later paraffin was used as fuel. Before the invention of matches, tinder boxes were used to light lamps and candles. A flint struck a steel plate, causing a spark to fall into the dry tinder (charred linen, for example) which burned.

Argand reading lamp, 1780s

Tinderbox, 1700s

Matches 1800s

Gas lamp 1840s

Edison lamp, 1879

Fluorescent tube

The hissing gas lamp was replaced by electric light after the 1880s. Edison's and Swan's pioneer bulb was the forerunner of today's fluorescent tubes and tungsten-filament lamps.

Tungsten bulb, 1911

Keeping Warm – Keeping Clean

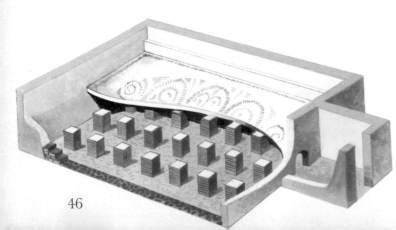

▲ Inside the boiling room of a 19th-century soap works. Tallow, vegetable oil and caustic soda were boiled in large vats. The liquid soap was skimmed off, dried and cut into bars.

▶ Umbrellas were probably invented as sunshades by the ancient Chinese and Greeks. As a protection against rain, they were still an unusual sight in the 1700s.

▼ In the Roman hypocaust, hot air circulated beneath the raised floor. Smoke escaped through flues built into the walls.

Until fairly recently, the only way people kept themselves warm was through thick clothes and open fires. Up to the 1300s houses had no chimneys either – smoke merely drifted out through a hole in the roof. Few houses had glass over the windows.

Open hearth fires or closed wood and coal stoves were the most common form of heating until the 1870s. Then gas fires appeared, using a burner developed by Baron Bunsen in the 1850s. Paraffin and electric fires came later and, like gas fires, they are still in use today.

Central Heating

Two thousand years ago the Romans heated their public baths by circulating hot air under the floors. In 1624 Lois Savot used a similar principle to heat the Louvre in Paris. Air warmed behind a fire was let into the rooms through a vent.

Later, with the development of hot water heating, central heating was further investigated. Today most offices, factories and homes are heated in this way using oil, gas, or electricity as fuel, and air can be conditioned – cleaned, cooled or warmed – before it enters a building.

Washing

At Mohenjo Daro, an ancient city in India, there are remains of modern-looking drains and lavatories – 4500 years old. The palaces of Crete also had piped fresh water for washing and drinking. Soap was used in ancient Sumeria. But it was unknown to the Romans, for whom bathing was an important social event. They oiled their bodies and scraped themselves clean.

In Europe people hardly washed themselves at all right up to the 1800s. There were few drains and little piped water. Often they used to perfume their bodies to disguise the smell. Open sewers with their danger to health eventually led to the building of closed drains and improved water supplies in towns.

Cleaning the house was hard work, often only done if one had plenty of servants armed with mops and brooms. But soon inventors came up with ideas to help with the work. The mechanical carpet sweeper (1876) was soon followed by the hand-cranked vacuum cleaner, worked by bellows. In 1901 Hubert Booth added an electric motor and an air filter. The first washing machines, built in the 1860s were worked by turning a handle. By 1914 motors had been fitted, and in the 1920s spin driers appeared. Detergents, invented in 1916, came into general use after 1945.

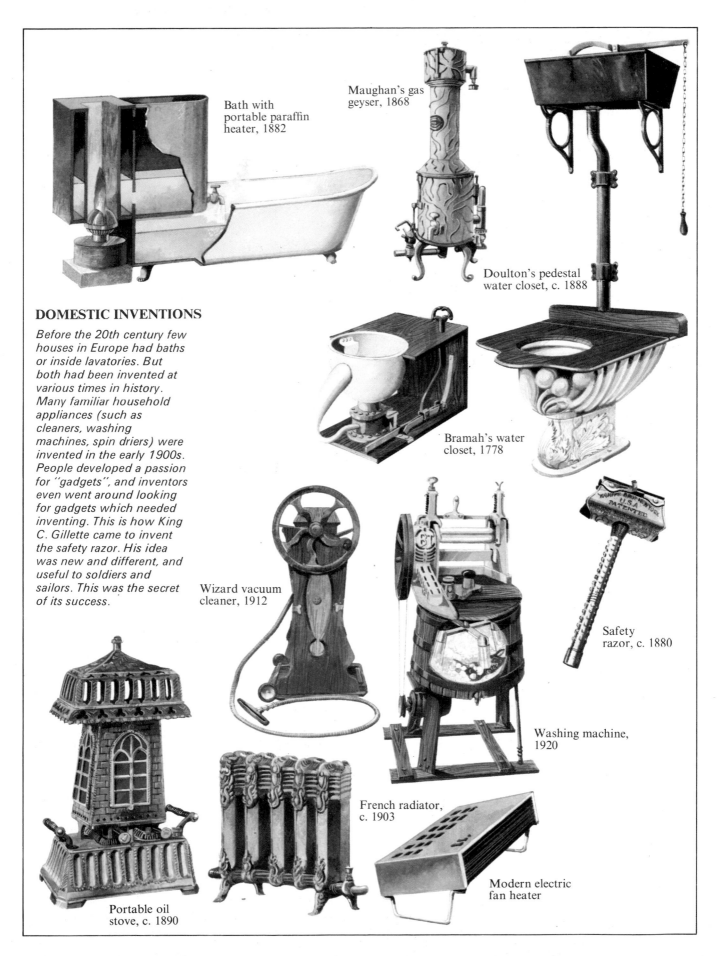

Bath with portable paraffin heater, 1882

Maughan's gas geyser, 1868

Doulton's pedestal water closet, c. 1888

Bramah's water closet, 1778

DOMESTIC INVENTIONS

Before the 20th century few houses in Europe had baths or inside lavatories. But both had been invented at various times in history. Many familiar household appliances (such as cleaners, washing machines, spin driers) were invented in the early 1900s. People developed a passion for "gadgets", and inventors even went around looking for gadgets which needed inventing. This is how King C. Gillette came to invent the safety razor. His idea was new and different, and useful to soldiers and sailors. This was the secret of its success.

Wizard vacuum cleaner, 1912

Safety razor, c. 1880

Washing machine, 1920

French radiator, c. 1903

Portable oil stove, c. 1890

Modern electric fan heater

► Whitcomb Judson's original zip fastener (1893). It was improved by Gideon Sundback of Sweden (1913).

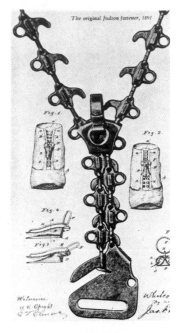

The original Judson fastener, 1891

◄ Isaac Singer developed Thimmonier's sewing machine idea. This Singer machine was made in 1851.

▼ A silver-gilt pin, made about 400 AD. Similar pins were used to fasten clothing throughout the ancient world. The modern safety pin, with a loop spring, was developed in the 1940s.

Clothing

Unlike most mammals, man has very little hair on his body. So he needs clothes to keep him warm. Man's first clothes were made from the fur or hide of animals he killed for food.

When man became a tool-maker, he cut and sewed skins into clothes (see page 11). Later, when he had become a farmer, he spun the wool from sheep and goats into yarn and wove cloth. He learned how to spin and weave the fibers of plants, such as flax. Cotton was made into cloth in India over 5000 years ago, and the Chinese were making silk at about the same time. The "silk route" from Europe to China became one of the most important trade routes in history.

This was because, from earliest times, clothing was a mark of a person's rank. Rulers wore fine robes, and decorated themselves with cosmetics and jewelry. Europeans were particularly eager for fine fabrics, such as silk, damask (from Damascus, Syria) and muslin (from Mosul, Iraq).

The ancient Greeks fastened their clothing with metal brooches and pins. Buttons were made from shells, stones, wood or bones as early as 3000 BC.

Factory-made metal buttons appeared in the late 1700s, and the first zip fastener was invented in 1891 by Whitcomb Judson.

Until modern times many people went barefoot, even in winter. In ancient Rome cobblers made leather shoes and sandals by cutting round the outline of the customer's foot. Trousers were worn in pre-Roman Britain and also in China. Stockings as we know them today developed from the long hose or breeches worn in the Middle Ages.

The past 500 years have seen many changes in fashion. Often fashion trends have made clothes more decorative but less practical. All clothes were made by hand until the Industrial Revolution, when factory-made clothing became cheap enough for most people to afford. Home dress-making became popular in the 1800s, after the introduction of the sewing machine (1830) and paper patterns (1863).

But perhaps the most important development has been the introduction of man-made textiles. The first of these was rayon, invented by Hilaire de Chardonnet in 1884. The discovery of nylon (1936) and Terylene (1941) followed. Natural fibers such as cotton and wool can be "finished" with chemicals to make them crease-proof.

► *Egyptians playing a board game with ivory pieces. Most board games mimic the actions of armies in battle, or of hunter and prey.*

▲ *Ball games, dice and counter games and terra cotta models were favourites in Egyptian times. The china doll dates from the 1800s.*

▼ *A Sumerian board game dating from 2600 BC.*

▼ *Tarot cards, bottom, were included in a pack of cards in the Middle Ages.*

XVIIII

LE·SOLEIL

VII

LE CHARIOT

Entertainment

Children's games such as Blind Man's Buff, Five-stones and Tag have been played for centuries. Throwing and catching games were played at first with balls made from skin stuffed with moss. Roman children played marbles, and in China and Japan kites have been popular with children and adults for thousands of years.

At the first Olympic Games in 776 BC, Greek athletes competed in horse, chariot and running races, wrestling, boxing and discus and javelin throwing. The Greeks also enjoyed tug-of-war contests and played a game rather like hockey. The Romans too liked ball games and also gambling with dice. But their favorite sports were gladiator combats and violent chariot races.

Central Asian horsemen played a wild form of polo, using a prisoner's head as the ball. Village football in the Middle Ages was almost as rough. English kings tried to ban football, so that people would spend more time practising archery. Noblemen scorned such games, preferring hunting, hawking and tournament jousting. The original rules for most of the games we play today were drawn up in the 1800s. Examples are soccer (1863), lawn tennis (1873) and hockey (1886).

Almost every ancient people played some form of board game, using stones, bones or shells. Most board games mimic the actions of hunting or war. Chess originated in India before 500 AD and reached Europe by way of the Arabs. Playing cards were a Chinese invention.

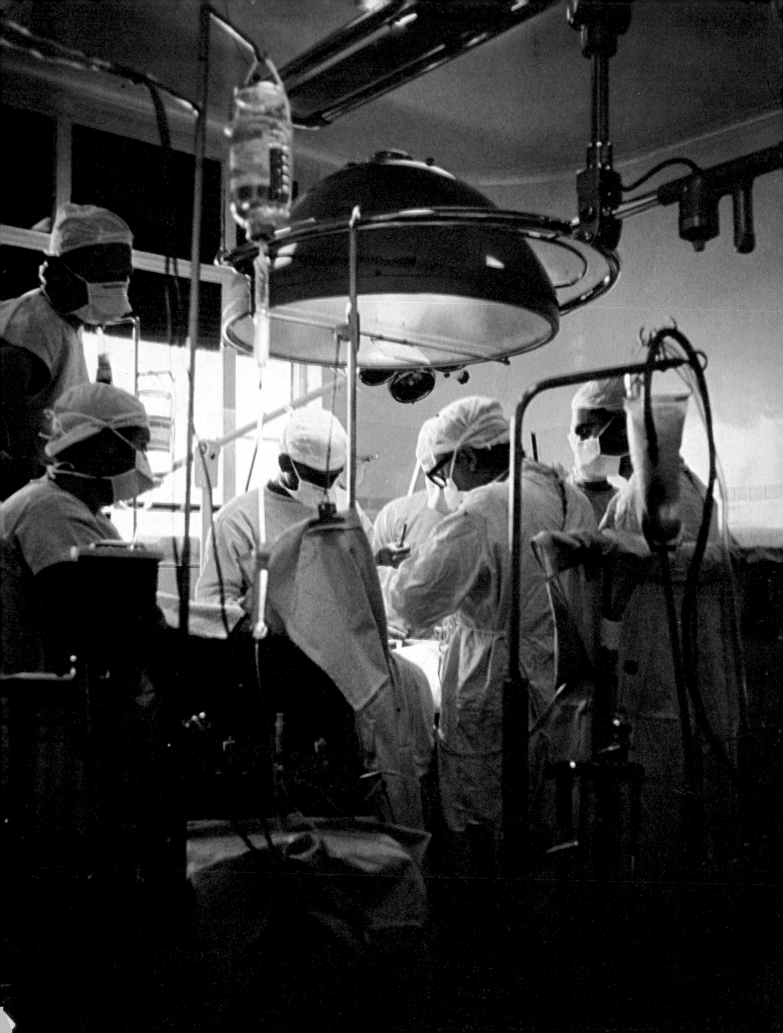

Chapter Six

The Story of Medicine

◀ Surgeons at work in a modern operating theatre.

▲ With this microscope, Hooke discovered the cell.

Prehistoric people made medicines from plants and berries. They also attempted surgery. Primitive medicine was mixed up with religion and magic. Doctors were also priests and magicians, using spells as "cures".

In the Middle Ages there were few hospitals, mostly run by monks and nuns. Barber-surgeons pulled teeth as well as cutting hair. Doctors were often ignorant "quacks" selling false cures and medicines.

No-one knew what caused disease, because there were no scientific tools to help doctors understand the body's secrets. One of the first, and most important, medical instruments was the microscope. With its help, doctors could learn more about anatomy (how the body is made) and physiology (how the body works). By dissecting animals and then human bodies, scientists could also study parts of the body and observe the effects of disease.

The ancient Egyptians and Jews knew that good food and cleanliness were vital for "public health". But dirt and poor hygiene remained the doctor's enemies until the 1800s. Only slowly was it realized that better housing, good sanitation, improved childcare and a proper attention to diet could prevent people from becoming ill.

Today most countries have a health service with hospitals, dental surgeries and clinics. Doctors, nurses and dentists are trained to use advanced machinery and sophisticated drugs

Thanks to the work of the World Health Organization, once deadly diseases such as smallpox have been conquered. Other diseases such as cancer still await a cure, and much remains to be done, especially in poorer countries.

The First Healers

When primitive people fell ill, they thought they were the victims of magic. Witchdoctors used spells and charms to drive out the "evil spirits" of sickness. Certain plants, they discovered, helped cure the sick. These herbs were the first medicines.

The First Doctors

More than 3000 years ago Chinese doctors used acupuncture and herbal drugs, while in India surgeons carried out skillful eye, bladder and even skin-grafting operations. In ancient Egypt doctors were priests as well. They used splints and casts for broken bones and knew about medicines. But they also believed in magic.

Medicine and Magic

The Greeks learned more about the human body by cutting open corpses. The Greek doctor Hippocrates (born 460 BC) is often called the "Father of Medicine". He taught doctors to observe and record symptoms in patients in a scientific manner. Another Greek, called Galen, was famous in Roman times. He followed the medical teachings of the time that sickness was caused by some upset of four mysterious liquids or "humors" which made up the body. Blood letting was very common as a cure for many illnesses.

The theory of the humors was wrong. But everyone accepted the idea and, during the Middle Ages, medicine stood still. The Church opposed dissection of human bodies. Alchemists wasted their time trying to find the magical "Elixir of Life" which they thought would cure all diseases. Plague and smallpox ravaged Europe, killing thousands of people, but doctors could do little to help.

New Discoveries

However, the Arabs preserved much of the medical knowledge of the past. And, during the Renaissance, scientists began to question the old, muddled ideas. They began to study the body, and invented new tools, such as the microscope (1590) to help them search for the causes of disease.

Leonardo da Vinci, Vesalius and Paré dissected bodies in order to learn about the anatomy and how the human body worked. Their work was very useful to later physicians such as William Harvey who, in 1619, discovered that blood was pumped around the body by the heart. Gradually from the 1600s medicine became more and more of a science.

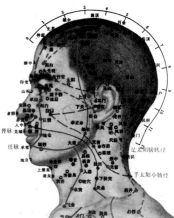

◀ Louis Pasteur (center) at his clinic. In 1885 he successfully inoculated a child bitten by a rabid dog.

▼ Acupuncture is an ancient Chinese medical treatment, in which needles are inserted into any of 365 special points on the body.

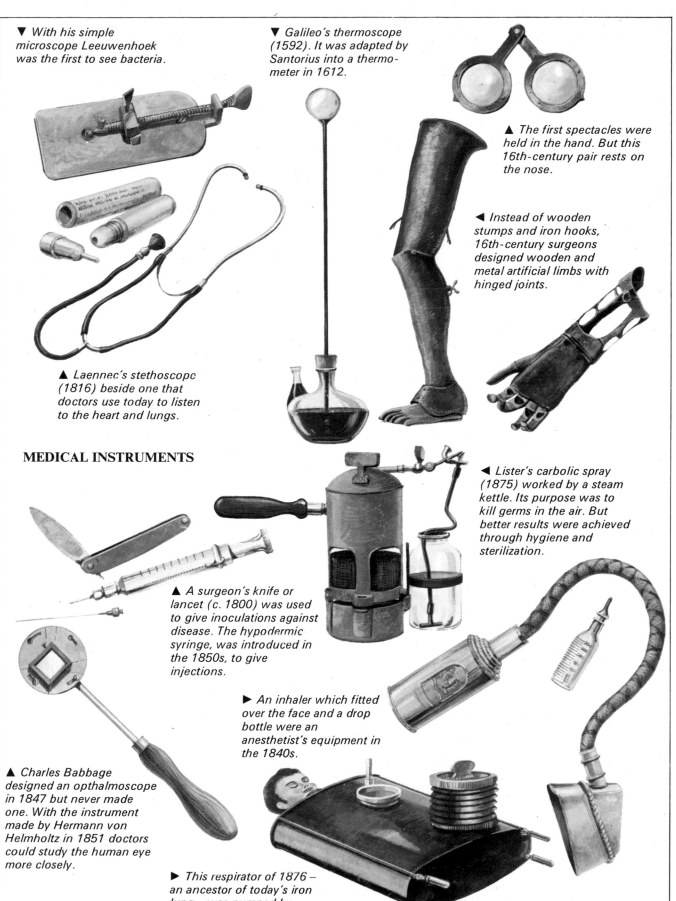

▼ With his simple microscope Leeuwenhoek was the first to see bacteria.

▼ Galileo's thermoscope (1592). It was adapted by Santorius into a thermometer in 1612.

▲ The first spectacles were held in the hand. But this 16th-century pair rests on the nose.

◄ Instead of wooden stumps and iron hooks, 16th-century surgeons designed wooden and metal artificial limbs with hinged joints.

▲ Laennec's stethoscope (1816) beside one that doctors use today to listen to the heart and lungs.

MEDICAL INSTRUMENTS

◄ Lister's carbolic spray (1875) worked by a steam kettle. Its purpose was to kill germs in the air. But better results were achieved through hygiene and sterilization.

▲ A surgeon's knife or lancet (c. 1800) was used to give inoculations against disease. The hypodermic syringe, was introduced in the 1850s, to give injections.

► An inhaler which fitted over the face and a drop bottle were an anesthetist's equipment in the 1840s.

▲ Charles Babbage designed an opthalmoscope in 1847 but never made one. With the instrument made by Hermann von Helmholtz in 1851 doctors could study the human eye more closely.

► This respirator of 1876 – an ancestor of today's iron lung – was pumped by hand.

Medicine as a Science

Through study of the body, doctors learned more and more about how it worked. They discovered at the same time more about the ways in which diseases affected the body. But still the actual causes of disease baffled them.

Bacteria and Antiseptics

In 1683, Anton van Leeuwenhoek looked through a home-made microscope at a drop of canal water and found it crawling with tiny creatures. He was the first to see what we call bacteria.

For a long time scientists could find no reason for the appearance of these creatures. They seemed to create themselves from nothing. But in the 1850s Louis Pasteur discovered that tiny creatures were present everywhere in the air. He called them "germs" and discovered that they could be killed by heat. The milk that we drink today is cleaned of germs by a process called pasteurization after Pasteur. Until this discovery, no-one thought that dirt had anything to do with disease. Hospitals were dirty, wounds were not cleaned, and as a result bacteria and infection thrived.

Joseph Lister showed that harmful bacteria could be killed with "antiseptics" such as carbolic. Infection could be prevented by sterilizing (boiling) all surgical instruments. Better hygiene, closed drains, and purer water supplies helped doctors fight disease.

◄ Rembrandt's painting 'The Anatomy Lesson' shows the 17th-century Dutch anatomist Nicolaas Tulp. Grave-robbers often supplied corpses for anatomists to dissect.

▲ William Morton giving ether to a patient. Morton, an American dentist, began using ether as an anaesthetic in 1846.

► Vesalius (1514–64) was the first great anatomist. He dissected human bodies and made careful drawings of what he saw.

Vaccines and Antibiotics

The Arabs had discovered that if someone caught a mild dose of a disease, he became "immune" or protected from a more serious attack later. During a smallpox outbreak in the 1790s, Edward Jenner deliberately injected a boy with cowpox (a similar, but mild disease). This "vaccination" protected the boy from smallpox. Koch and Pasteur developed Jenner's discovery and today there are vaccines to guard us against many diseases.

In the 1900s doctors discovered even smaller creatures than germs, called viruses. Viruses cause many diseases, including colds and 'flu. To kill viruses, new drugs were developed. Among the most useful drugs are antibiotics. The first antibiotic was discovered by Alexander Fleming in 1928. He found that mold growing on a specimen taken from a patient had killed the germs. He called this mold penicillin. But it took eleven years before this discovery was perfected.

Probing the Mind

From the 1800s the way the brain worked was studied by many physicians. Among these was Sigmund Freud who began by studying the nervous system which carries out the commands of the brain. He found out that dreams gave valuable information about what goes on in the deeper parts of the mind and invented what he called "free association" to help people remember their dreams. This formed the basis of psychoanalysis and paved the way for later research into the cause of mental illness.

X-Rays and Transplants

Early doctors could only guess at what was wrong inside their patients. But with the stethoscope, invented by René Laennec in 1816, doctors could listen to a person's heart and lungs. With X-rays, discovered by Wilhelm von Roentgen in 1895, they could take photographs of a person's insides. This made possible great steps forward in surgery.

Until the 1800s surgery was performed with only alcohol and herbs to kill the pain. Many patients died of shock, until the introduction of the first anesthetics (ether, 1842 and chloroform, 1847). Today, surgeons can "transplant" organs such as kidneys from healthy people to sick people. Machines such as the heart-lung machine (1929) and the kidney machine (1944) can do the work of diseased organs and keep people alive.

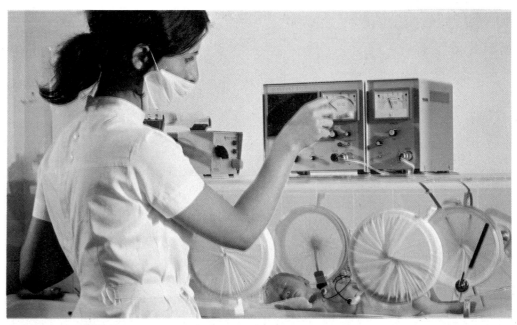

▲ Before the days of anesthetics and high-speed drills, a visit to the dentist was a painful business, as this drawing of an 18th-century French dentist at work clearly shows. People suffering from toothache eased the pain with laudanum. Aspirin was not developed until 1899.

◄ Advanced machines in today's hospitals, such as this incubator, often save lives. Here a premature baby is cared for in a warm, germ-free environment. Tiny devices fixed to the child continually check his heartbeat and breathing and warn of any changes in his condition.

Chapter Seven
Wheels, Wings and Sails

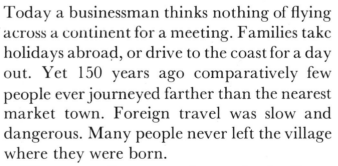

◄ Traffic jams, like this one on a Brazilian highway are common all over the world.

▲ One of the pioneers of flight, Otto Lilienthal flew in his glider in the 1890s.

Today a businessman thinks nothing of flying across a continent for a meeting. Families take holidays abroad, or drive to the coast for a day out. Yet 150 years ago comparatively few people ever journeyed farther than the nearest market town. Foreign travel was slow and dangerous. Many people never left the village where they were born.

The story of transport began in the Stone Age. Someone discovered that wood would float, and in time people learned to make rafts and dugout canoes. The use of tree trunks as rollers to help move heavy stones led to the invention of the wheel. We do not know who invented the wheel. But carts with wheels cut from tree trunks were used in the Near East more than 5000 years ago.

Later, in sailing ships, explorers crossed the seas to discover new lands. Trade developed. Navigation improved. But land travel changed very slowly. Until the 1700s no-one had ever traveled faster than a horse could run. Then came the Industrial Revolution and the Age of Machines.

Now speed became important for trade. A transport race began. Among the most important inventions were the balloon (1783), the steamship (1807), the steam railroad (1830), the motor car (1885), and the airplane (1903). Travel became faster and simpler, and changed people's way of life.

In the 20th century many people in the richer countries enjoy the luxury of personal transport by car. They also use advanced public transport systems. In poorer countries horses, oxen and camels still carry people and goods. Yet supersonic jets circle the world in a few hours. As the Earth shrinks, rockets have given us a new dream – of travel into space, to new worlds.

On the Road

The first roads were tracks worn by the plodding feet of men and pack animals. The only land vehicle was the sledge, until the invention of the wheel around 5000 years ago.

Oxen and Horses

The first carts had solid wooden wheels. Spoked wheels were invented around 2000 BC. At this time the fastest means of travel was by chariot. Chariots were drawn by horses and mainly used in battle. Carts were developed for farm work and were very slow. For a long time they were pulled by oxen. Oxen could pull heavier loads than horses. The yoke harness tended to choke a horse, and this problem was not solved until the invention of the rigid horse collar in the Middle Ages.

For horse-riding, the bridle and saddle were very early inventions. Stirrups came later, reaching Europe from the East about 800 AD.

Carriages and Coaches

During the Middle Ages in Europe, people travelled on horseback or in horse-drawn two-wheeled carriages. Huge wagons pulled by up to 12 horses were used to transport goods. By the 1470s, four-wheeled carriages had been introduced. As roads improved, stage coaches began to carry people from town to town, changing horses at each stop (usually at an inn). Gradually the design of coaches and smaller carriages improved. Leather suspension straps and later springs gave passengers a more comfortable ride and glass windows helped keep out the wind and rain.

Steam Carriages and Horse Trams

The first person to make a steam engine drive a wheeled vehicle was a Frenchman called Nicolas Cugnot. His steam carriage (1769) was very slow. But other inventors took up the idea. In 1801 Richard Trevithick drove a steam carriage around his Cornish village, and in 1804 Oliver Evans drove a steam-powered dredging machine fitted with wheels through the streets of Philadelphia.

By the 1830s Sir Goldsworthy Gurney's steam coaches were carrying passengers at the alarming speed of 25 km/h (15 mph). Other road-users complained that horses bolted at the sight and sound of a steam engine, and in 1865 a law was

(Continued on page 60)

The horse was not only a beast of burden. It could also be a mark of rank. The elegant Chinese carriage and the lavish medieval harness proved their owners to be men of importance.

58

► Cugnot's three-wheeled steam carriage was intended to pull heavy cannon. Its top speed was only just over 3 km/h (2 mph) but it was the first working motor vehicle.

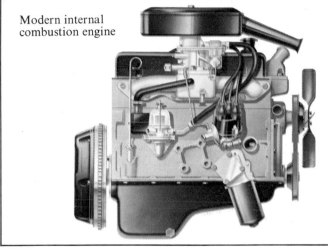

Modern internal combustion engine

The Car-builders

A car engine has more than 150 moving parts. Machine tools and skilled mechanics were needed to make and fit the parts together. Most early cars were built by hand in small workshops. The first car-makers built their own engines. They also made gearboxes, clutches, differentials (to make the outside wheels turn faster than the inside wheels while the car is cornering), and the car's other systems – brakes, electrical, steering, suspension, fuel and cooling. They combined the skills of the coachmaker and railroad engineer, and added some new ones of their own. Mass production of cars, using assembly lines and conveyor belts, began in the 1900s. Instead of building a complete car from start to finish, a worker now performed just one task such as tightening bolts on the wheels. This is a faster and cheaper method of car-building.

The horse-drawn omnibus first appeared in France around 1825, and in London open-top horse buses remained in use until 1916. The Benz Velo of 1893 had a 3½ h.p. engine. It was the first car to be built in quantity.

The first cars, with their spoked wheels and complete absence of protection against the weather or accident, look quaint compared with a modern saloon such as the Wankel-engined Japanese Mazda.

passed in Britain slowing all "horseless carriages" to a maximum speed of only 6 km/h (4 mph). Until this law was abolished in 1896 a man with a red flag had to walk in front to warn people of the approach of such dangerous vehicles.

Although "road locomotives" did not catch on, another idea borrowed from the railroads was a success. Metal rails were laid in city streets and trams, pulled by horses, ran along them. Steam trams appeared in the 1860s, and the first electric tram (which picked up current from overhead wires) in 1901 (see page 63).

The Bicycle

In the early 1800s fashionable young men took to riding "dandy-horses". These machines looked like bicycles, but had no pedals. The rider pushed himself along with his feet. In 1839 Kirkpatrick Macmillan built a bicycle driven by pedals attached to the front wheel. But the new machine did not catch the public fancy until 1861 when the Michaux velocipede or "bone-shaker" appeared.

To provide some form of gearing, the front wheel of the bicycle was at first made very large. This trend led to the famous "penny-farthing ordinary" bicycle of the 1870s. But with the designing of chain drive (1879) and pneumatic rubber tires (1888), the bicycle took on the look of the machine we know today.

Automobile

From the 1860s several engineers were working on internal combustion engines burning gas or petroleum as fuel. The breakthrough came with Nikolaus Otto's four-stroke gasoline engine of 1876. This type of engine was used in the first motor cars built in the mid 1880s by Karl Benz and Gottfried Daimler. Daimler also fitted an engine to a bicycle to make the first motor cycle (1885) but it was never produced. The first motor cycles to be manufactured were made by Hildebrande and Wolfmüller in the 1890s.

Electric and steam cars were both tried, with some success. An electric car set the first world land speed record in 1898 – at 63 km/h. And in 1904 a steam car was driven at over 160 km/h (100 mph). But electric cars ran only as long as their batteries lasted (not long in the early 1900s), while steam cars had to carry heavy loads of fuel and water and also needed cleaning out regularly. Gasoline engines were more complicated. But their greater power and reliability won the day – although today, as the world faces a petroleum

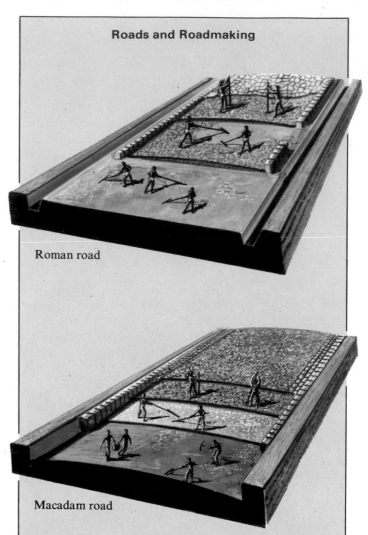

Roads and Roadmaking

Roman road

Macadam road

The first paved roads suitable for wheeled carts were built by the Babylonians 4,000 years ago. But the first great road builders were the Romans. Their roads were made from stones and gravel, and mostly ran in a straight line. The road surface was cambered (sloped from the middle to the edge) so that water drained off easily.

On their good roads the Romans could march quickly to deal with revolts within their empire. But merchants also used the roads, so trade flourished. After the Roman Empire collapsed, these roads were neglected and a road journey was often a dangerous adventure. Attempts were made from time to time to repair old roads and build new ones. But not much was done until the Industrial Revolution when more goods had to be carried to and from the new factories.

Thomas Telford (1757–1834) and John McAdam (1756–1836) worked on this problem. Telford's roads, like the Roman roads, had solid stone foundations. McAdam's roads were made from layers of small stones topped by small stones. Stamped down by road workers and ground together by heavy cart wheels passing over them, these made a hard surface.

A further change came with the invention of bicycles, motor cycles and motor cars in the 1800s. The new machines, with their air-filled rubber tires, needed a less gritty road surface. The answer was to coat the road with a skin of small stones mixed with bitumen or tar and roll it flat. This 'tarmacadam' surface is waterproof and very tough.

Bicycles and Motorcycles

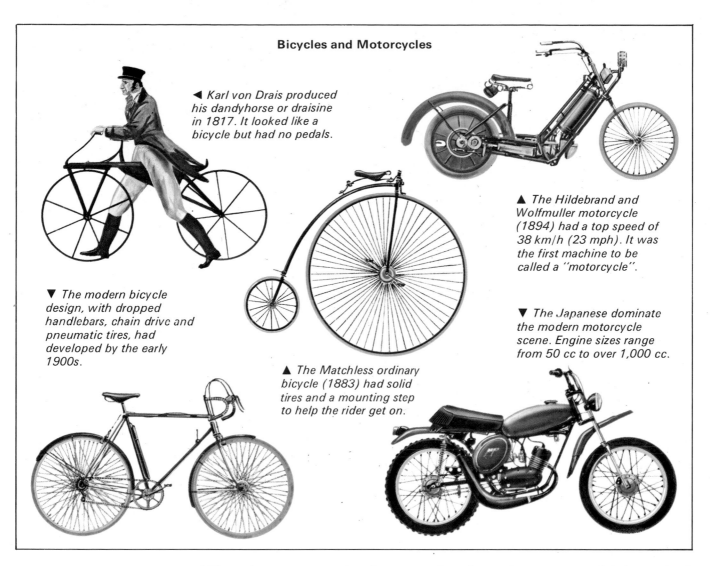

◄ *Karl von Drais produced his dandyhorse or draisine in 1817. It looked like a bicycle but had no pedals.*

▼ *The modern bicycle design, with dropped handlebars, chain drive and pneumatic tires, had developed by the early 1900s.*

▲ *The Matchless ordinary bicycle (1883) had solid tires and a mounting step to help the rider get on.*

▲ *The Hildebrand and Wolfmuller motorcycle (1894) had a top speed of 38 km/h (23 mph). It was the first machine to be called a "motorcycle".*

▼ *The Japanese dominate the modern motorcycle scene. Engine sizes range from 50 cc to over 1,000 cc.*

◄ *The cat's eye, invented by Percy Shaw in 1934, is a simple but effective road-marker. The glass "eyes" reflect light from oncoming headlights. The rubber casing protects the eyes and wipes them clean every time a car passes over them.*

◄ *John Dunlop, a Scottish vet, invented the pneumatic (air-filled) rubber tire for his son's tricycle. Previously most wheels had had solid rubber, wooden or iron rims.*

◄ *All bicycles were driven by pedals connected to the front wheel until the development of a strong but flexible drive chain by Hans Renold in the 1880s. Chain drive made gearing possible, and large front wheels were no longer necessary for high speeds.*

shortage, electric and steam cars begin to look interesting once more.

The first automobiles still looked very like horsedrawn carriages, with their plush upholstery, spoked wheels, brass lamps and external brake levers. Often the driver sat in the open, in front of the passenger compartment. Motoring quickly became popular with the well-to-do. And when mass production of cars in factories began in the early 1900s, a transport revolution was under way. Henry Ford's "tin lizzie", the famous Model T of 1908, was the first cheap, family car.

Since then the automobile has become faster and more complicated. Trucks and buses are often powered by diesel engines, invented by Rudolf Diesel in 1893. (A diesel engine is ignited by the heat of compressed air rather than by an electrical spark.) Another development is the rotary engine invented by Felix Wankel in 1956. The automobile has become the most important means of personal transport used in the 20th century. It has changed the look, sound and smell of our cities.

Traveling by Rail

In the 1500s engineers knew that a heavy wagon would move more easily on rails. Wooden railways were used in mines to transport coal. As there were no engines, the wagons were pulled by horses or men.

Steam engines were invented in the 1700s. At first they were used only to drive water pumps. In 1801 a Cornish engineer called Richard Trevithick fitted a steam engine with wheels. His "steam carriage" worked, and he drove it on the roads. In 1804 he built a better "locomotive" which ran on rails.

The Railroad Age
It was George Stephenson who realized the importance of Trevithick's invention. He built bigger, faster locomotives such as the *Rocket* (1829). In 1830 he opened the world's first all-steam railroad, between Liverpool and Manchester.

Soon railroads were being built all over the world. Tunnels were driven through mountains. Railroad bridges spanned rivers. The first railroad across the United States was completed in 1869. Semaphore signals, invented by Chappé in 1791, were introduced to improve rail safety and steel rails were successfully used in 1862. In 1863 the world's first underground railroad was opened in London. The trains were steam driven.

From Steam to Electric
The first electric train was demonstrated in 1879. By the 1890s trams on rails had become a common sight in city streets. But steam power continued to reign supreme and huge locomotives were built in the 1930s and 40s.

However, by the 1970s few steam-driven locomotives were still in use. Electric and diesel trains – cleaner, faster, and more efficient – had replaced them.

The Importance of Railroads
The railroads speeded up the Industrial Revolution and carried settlers to new lands. For the first time ordinary people could travel long distances quite cheaply.

Today railroads are less important. The car is more convenient and the airplane is faster. Many railroads have been closed. But railroads are still useful and underground railroads are essential in car-cluttered cities. In the future, express trains using the air cushion or magnetic lift principles will be able to reach speeds of over 400 km/hr (250 mph).

▼ George Stephenson's "Rocket" won the 1829 trials to find the fastest locomotive for the Liverpool and Manchester Railway – the world's first all-steam public railroad. With its multiple-tube boiler, the "Rocket" managed a top speed of 58 km/h (36 mph).

▶ Passengers at Baker Street Station, London, where in 1863 the first underground railroad was opened. The line was built by the "cut and cover" method (rather than by driving deep tunnels), and the first locomotives were steam engines.

▼ The first successful diesel locomotives were built in Germany in 1932. Today diesel freight trains can weigh up to 15,000 tons.

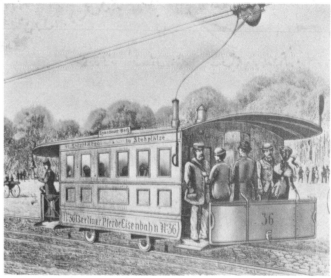

▼ Modern streamlining, the use of high-power electric and gas turbine engines, and improved suspension for taking bends at speed make it possible for some trains to reach speeds of over 200 km/h (125 mph).
▶ Von Siemen's electric tram in Berlin (1881). It picked up current from overhead wires.

Across the Oceans

People made boats long before they could draw or write. The first boat was probably a floating log. Primitive people then discovered how to make rafts by fastening logs or bundles of reeds together. They hollowed out tree trunks to make canoes, and, much later, they learned to make use of the wind by means of a mast and a square sail.

The first seagoing ships sailed the Mediterranean Sea about 6,000 years ago. The Phoenicians, who were famous sailors, had slow ships for trade and fast slender galleys for battle. Galleys relied mainly on oars for speed. The Vikings used oars and sails and managed to cross the Atlantic Ocean in their longships.

The Age of Sail

During the Middle Ages sails and rigging became more complicated. Around 1200 the stern rudder replaced the steering oar, allowing the helmsman to steer more accurately. By 1400 the three-masted carrack combined the best features of ship design in northern and southern Europe.

In these improved ships European explorers made long voyages of discovery, beginning in the 1400s. Navigation methods also improved with inventions such as the astrolabe (1500s), the log-line (1590s), the sextant (1730s) and the chronometer (1760s). Extra sails were added, and in the 1850s sailing ships reached a peak with the fast clippers. But by then steam was taking over.

From Paddle Steamers to Super Tankers

In 1783 the Marquis Jouffroy d'Abbans tried his steamer operated by paddles. By 1807 the first commercially successful steamship was working on the Hudson River. An iron ship was built in 1818, and soon metal was being used to build most ships. Early steamships had paddlewheels, but from 1836 screw propellers came into use. Ships became larger, with more powerful engines, such as the steam turbine, first used in a ship in 1894.

In the early 1900s the ocean liner was queen of the seas. Today ocean giants are oil tankers, container ships and other cargo vessels. In the 1950s a few nuclear-powered ships, capable of sailing around the world without refueling were developed. More recently hydrofoils and hovercraft have come into use for shorter journeys. They can travel faster than ordinary ships because they skim over the surface of the water.

▲ Navigation buoys were used as early as 1000. This example dates from the 1880s. Many modern buoys look like this, but have radar beacons and electronic aids for even greater safety.

▲ The Eddystone lighthouse (1759) designed by John Smeaton was a guide to sailors in the Atlantic for over 100 years.

Backstaff

▶ The compass invented by the ancient Chinese was rediscovered by European sailors in the 12th century. By the 1600s sailors were using a backstaff to find out their position and a log line to gauge their speed. By inserting pegs at half hour intervals in a traverse board, they could calculate how far they had traveled, in one direction.

Compass

Traverse board

BOATS AND SHIPS

▶ Log rafts were usually pushed along with the aid of a long pole.

▲ Dug-out canoes were fairly easy to paddle.

▼ Egyptian ships had no keel and were kept rigid by a hogging line tied tightly from bow to stern. The ship was steered by oars.

▲ A carrack of the 1400s still had the raised stern and forecastle, originally used as fighting platforms.

◀ A paddle steamer of the 1800s. Early steamships had sails as well as engines, because they could not carry enough coal.

▲ The "United States" (1952) was the last holder of the Blue Riband for trans-Atlantic liners. She was capable of a speed of over 35 knots.

▼ The hovercraft's flexible "skirt" traps compressed air beneath the hull and increases the lift. The SRN4 ferry can travel over land or water, at speeds of up to 60 knots.

▶ David Bushnell's "Turtle" was the first military submarine. In 1776 the tiny screw-propelled one-man craft tried to sink a British warship by screwing explosive charges into the wooden hull.

In the Air

From earliest times people dreamed of being able to fly like the birds. A few intrepid inventors strapped on wings and jumped off towers. But the birdmen's attempts to fly ended in failure. For no-one yet understood the principles of flight.

Floating Flight

Man's conquest of the air began in 1783 when the Montgolfier brothers sent up a hot-air balloon. Later balloons were filled with hydrogen gas or helium, a gas discovered in 1895.

Henri Giffard's cigar-shaped steerable airship (1852) had a steam engine driving a propeller. But steam engines were too heavy for aircraft. Gasoline engines, being smaller and lighter, were used in the successful Zeppelin airships of the early 1900s, which could carry passengers across the Atlantic. However, in the 1930s a series of crashes brought the airship story to a close.

From Gliders to Flyers

In 1804 Sir George Cayley's model glider proved that a heavier-than-air machine would fly. In 1853 Cayley sent his terrified coachman aloft in a full-sized glider.

Otto Lilienthal experimented with a large kite-like glider in the 1890s, and his flights inspired the Wright brothers in America. On December 17, 1903 the Wrights' "Flyer" airplane made the first controlled and powered man-carrying flight.

Progress in Aviation

Airplane development was rapid. Newspapers offered prizes for record-breaking flights. In 1909 Blériot won a prize for crossing the Channel and in

◀ Leonardo da Vinci's design for a helicopter. In the 1500s such a machine could not have been built.

▼ Today's busy airways are controlled by radar. Airport controllers tell approaching aircraft when it is safe to land.

▲ One of the first flights in a hot air balloon over the court of Versailles in 1783.

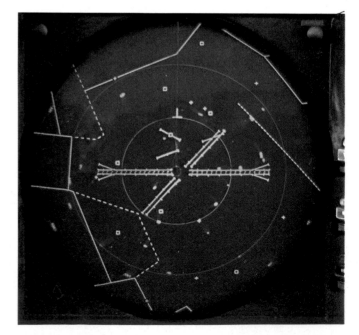

1927 Lindbergh flew solo non-stop from New York to Paris. During World War I metal monoplanes replaced the early fabric-covered biplanes.

Until the 1940s all airplanes had piston engines turning propellers. But propellers do not work well at great heights or at speeds above 800 km/h (500 mph). The first jet aircraft was the German Heinkel 178 (1939) and in the 1950s jets swiftly replaced piston propeller aircraft. Radar was first used during World War II, and the helicopter (1936) became a useful "work horse" of the air. By the 1970s "jumbo" jets, capable of carrying large numbers of people came into service.

Supersonic Speeds and Spaceflight

The first plane to fly faster than sound in level flight was the rocket-powered Bell X-1 (1947). During the 1970s supersonic airliners such as the Anglo-French Concorde and the Russian Tu-144 have brought huge cuts in traveling time on long distance flights.

The German V2 rocket of World War II was the forerunner of today's space rocket and the Space Age began when the Russians put the first artificial satellite (Sputnik I) in orbit around the Earth in 1957. Since then many artificial satellites have been launched. In 1961, a Russian, Yuri Gagarin, was the first man to circle the Earth and by 1969 American Apollo astronauts had landed on the Moon. Later, space laboratories were sent into space and unmanned probes were launched to explore other distant planets. In the 1980s the United States plans to operate a launching craft called a space shuttle which can be reused and so make space travel cheaper.

◄▲ *Wilbur Wright watches as his brother Orville makes the first powered and controlled flight in history (1903). It only lasted 12 seconds but by 1905 the Wrights were making flights lasting half an hour.*

▲ *The end of the Zeppelin "Hindenburg" in 1937. The huge airship was filled with highly flammable hydrogen gas.*

◄ *The Bell turbo-jet flying pack has hand controls for steering and adjusting power.*

▼ *The Apollo lunar module with its spidery landing legs catches the sun as it stands on the surface of the moon.*

Chapter Eight

War and Weapons

◄ *The Moguls besieging with a cannon and muskets an Indian city in 1571.*

▲ *Medieval knights jousting at a tournament.*

War is part of history. Since prehistoric times people have fought, to conquer new lands or to defend themselves against attack. Wars have brought destruction and suffering. But wars have also brought new ideas and discoveries.

In fact, the story of war is the story of invention. Each new weapon has been matched, sooner or later, by a new defense. Today we often speak of the "arms race" between the world's strongest nations. This arms race has been going on for thousands of years.

In ancient times battles were fought at close range, with hand-to-hand weapons such as clubs and swords, and throwing weapons, such as slings and spears. The bow was the first "missile launcher".

The first organized armies were those of ancient Egypt and Assyria, 3000 years ago. Battle tactics soon developed. Chariots and cavalry were early "shock weapons", while catapults were a primitive form of artillery.

War changed little until the discovery of explosives in the Middle Ages. This changed the pattern of warfare. For the gun made armored knights and stone-walled castles out-of-date.

Later, in the modern Age of Machines, inventions such as the railroad, telegraph, radio, submarine, airplane and radar made war even more deadly. In the 20th century two world wars inflicted huge losses on civilians as well as soldiers.

The modern army can fight on land, on sea and in the air, with the help of computers and robot weapons. Science has given us weapons so terrible they could destroy the world. These weapons, the guided missile and the hydrogen bomb, have created a "balance of fear" which, it is hoped, will maintain peace.

Early Warriors

The warriors of the ancient world fought mostly on foot, though chariots and horsemen grew in importance. The Egyptians wore little protection in battle except for helmets. Archers were armed with bows and arrows made of reed with heads of flint and later copper. Other soldiers were equipped with spears or the mace, a type of club.

Assyrian warriors wore long coats of mail. They developed many siege tactics and used battering rams to breach the walls of towns under siege. They were also expert archers.

Classical Warfare

Most battles were won by good tactics, rather than by better weapons. The Greeks made skillful use of the phalanx, a mass of spearmen protected behind a wall of shields. The Roman army was the best in the ancient world. Its strength lay in well-trained legions, good roads, strong forts, and siege weapons which included the ballista, an engine worked by ropes which hurled large stones.

The Middle Ages

The feudal system in which lords were given land by their king in return for protection was the foundation of the medieval army. Each lord had to raise an army from his estates to fight for the king. The use of stirrups (which kept him balanced while fighting) gave the horseman a greater advantage, and armored knights became the pride of medieval armies.

By the 1300s chain mail had given way to plate armor covering the whole of the knight's body. To defend their lands, lords built massive castles; so siege warfare was important. During a siege, the attacking army outside battered at the castle walls with siege engines which had changed little since Roman times. Soldiers tried to climb over the walls and tunnel under them, while the defenders fought back with a hail of arrows, spears, stones and boiling fat.

Attack and Defence

A knight's chief weapons were the mace, axe, war hammer, sword and lance. Foot soldiers fought off the horsemen with even longer halberds and pikes or, better still, with bows. The Welsh longbow could fire arrows through plate armor, and was a quicker-firing weapon than the crossbow, which had to be wound up for every shot.

▲ Assyrian archers used curved bows over 3000 years ago. Their long coats of mail protected them from their enemies.

▶ Besieging a castle in the Middle Ages.

◀ A basinet – a helmet that covered the whole head – was worn by knights in the Middle Ages.

▼ Spears, like the ones carried by the warriors on this Greek vase, are one of Man's oldest weapons. They were first tipped with stone, later with bronze and iron.

Gunpowder to Atom Bomb

Gunpowder rockets were invented by the ancient Chinese. But cannon were not used in battle until the 1300s. The first guns made a lot of noise, but did little damage.

Cannon and Muskets

However, improved cannon brought medieval warfare to an end, for knights and castles were helpless against artillery. Hand guns replaced bows and spears. First came the clumsy matchlock of the 1400s, then in the 1600s the more reliable flintlock musket.

Even so, armies seldom fought in wet weather, since their guns would not fire if the powder was damp. In the early 1800s the invention of a damp-proof firing cap solved this problem. Muskets fired solid lead balls and were loaded, rather slowly, from the muzzle end. The invention of cartridge ammunition, loaded from the breech, increased the rate of fire. Rifling (cutting spiral grooves inside the barrel) improved the range and accuracy of guns.

Mechanical Warfare

Explosive shells were used with devastating results in World War I. At sea steam "ironclads" had thick metal armor but they still had to watch out for mines and torpedoes. Armies could no longer advance in close ranks for rifle and machine gun fire mowed down the troops. Generals were slow to realize the importance of these changes. During World War I millions of men were killed trying to advance against gunfire and mortar bombs. Armies became bogged down in trenches. Only new weapons, such as the tank and the airplane could break the deadlock.

Bombs and Missiles

The ancient Greeks used flame throwers to set fire to enemy boats and towns. But the chemical incendiary bombs used in World War II were far more powerful. Whole cities were destroyed by air bombing. Yet unbelievably more destructive than any incendiary or high explosive were the atomic bombs, dropped on two Japanese cities, Hiroshima and Nagasaki in 1945 and the hydrogen bomb, first tested in 1952.

Guided missiles fired from aircraft, from submarines or from underground pits can carry such bombs for thousands of miles and hit a target with pin-point accuracy.

WEAPONS

► Early cannon were clumsy, inaccurate and frequently blew up when fired. Yet guns like "Mons Meg", cast in 1460, changed warfare.

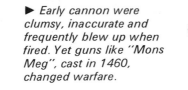

◄ Loading and firing a matchlock musket was an awkward and risky business. After loading with powder and ball, the musketeer set a glowing match to the touch-hole.

▼ The flintlock pistol. When the trigger was pulled, the flint in the cock struck a steel plate, and a spark fell into the priming pan. This "flash in the pan" set off the main charge.

▼ Gas masks were a necessary invention after poison gas was used in World War I.

▲ The Colt 45 revolver (1873). It had a revolving chamber and could fire six shots without reloading.

▲ The Gatling gun (1863) saw action in the U.S. Civil War. It had up to ten barrels, rotated by a hand crank.

▲ Some modern guided missiles are light enough to be carried by an infantryman. The Vigilant is a wire-guided rocket for destroying enemy tanks.

► The tank, crawling forward on caterpillar tracks, was an attempt to break the deadlock of trench warfare.

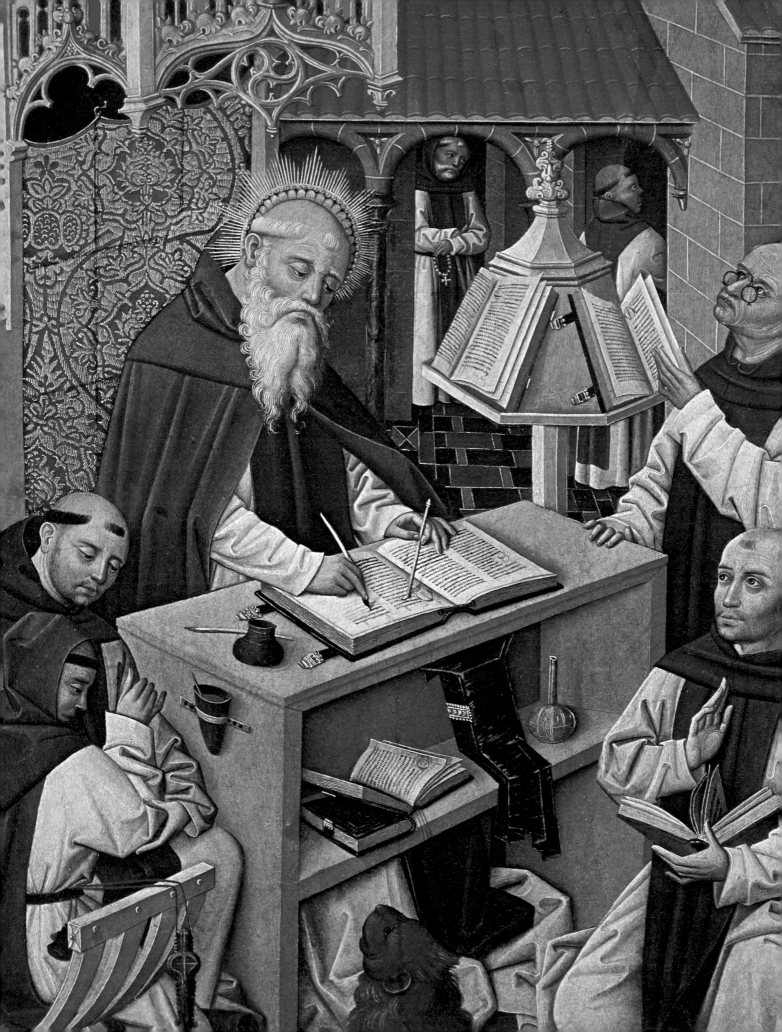

◄ *During the Middle Ages scribes in monasteries copied books by hand, using quill pens.*

▼ *Edison's phonograph. The records were cylindrical, and the horn amplified the sound.*

Chapter Nine

Communications

Communication is the transport of ideas. It is the way we learn. Civilization grew as ideas spread. From the time of the first Stone Age cave painters to today's mass media, such as radio, cinema and television, communications have changed the ways in which people think and behave.

No one knows when language began. Perhaps people first began to speak by imitating natural sounds such as bird cries or the sound of water. Certainly spoken language came thousands of years before writing. Information had to be passed on by word of mouth until the invention of the first writing – picture signs – over 5000 years ago. The development of writing meant that knowledge could be recorded in books and information passed on from generation to generation.

The development of numbers is almost as important as words. At first, people worked out a number system and simple weights and measures to help them weigh grain or measure land. Later mathematicians and astronomers devised calendars and learned how to calculate distance and time with more and more accuracy. Through their work people discovered more about the world and the universe beyond. Music, painting and other forms of art also enabled people to communicate ideas and feelings in new ways.

The last 500 years have produced two communications explosions. The printing revolution made books available to all. And in the last 100 years science has given us amazing new ways of message-sending and message-storing. Inventions such as photography, the telephone, sound recording, radio, television and computers, are the "keys" to the modern world. They give us instant communication. Information can be stored, and "called for" at the touch of a switch. And people's faces and voices can be recorded and preserved for ever.

The Story of Writing

Stone Age man wrote in pictures. We can still see his cave paintings, more than 25,000 years old. In time, instead of only drawing pictures of things, he also drew "picture-signs" to stand for ideas. For example, a picture of the sun meant "heat".

When people could draw picture-signs more quickly, they made them simpler, until the signs no longer looked like pictures at all. Picture-signs are called "ideographs" and among the most famous are the hieroglyphs of ancient Egypt.

Making an Alphabet

The next important step was to make signs stand for sounds or speech. This is called "phonetic writing". Writing in picture-signs means you need thousands of different characters, or pictures. (Chinese, for example, has 80,000 characters) With a simplified alphabet of sound-signs, you can group letters to make words.

The first alphabets were invented about 3,500 years ago. By borrowing letters, people made several alphabet "families". One family produced the Roman alphabet, from which comes the 26-letter alphabet we use today.

Pen and Ink

The first writing was "cuneiform" or wedge-shaped. People made signs by pressing a sharp tool into wet clay. Later, pens were made from grass or bamboo, although the Chinese preferred fine

▲ Written about 650 BC, this letter in cuneiform script on a wax tablet was carried inside a protective envelope probably by a messenger on horseback.

▲ Valentin Haüy (1771) used raised letters to teach blind people to read. Louis Braille's dot alphabet (1829) is widely used today. There are Braille typewriters and of course books printed in Braille.

◀ Chinese ink-makers preparing and mixing the ingredients (soot, oil, resin and gum). The Chinese began making ink around 2500 BC. It was made into blocks, since the Chinese wrote with paint brushes rather than with pens.

▲ Egyptian hieroglyphs were written on papyrus scrolls or on stones. No-one could read them until Jean François Champollion deciphered the Rosetta Stone in 1822.

► Konrad Gesner's pencil (1565) shown alongside modern ball point, fountain and felt tip pens.

▼ In a language laboratory tape-recorded lesson material is used to teach each pupil at his own pace.

brushes. Ink was used in Egyptian and Roman times. It was made from various substances, including soot, gum, iron, salt and cuttlefish!

After paper came into common use as a writing material in the Middle Ages people wrote with quill pens. Quills were the long tail or wing feathers of geese and other birds. The tip or nib of the quill was sharpened with a small pen knife. Lead sticks were used for writing in the 1500s. But wooden pencils with graphite "leads" did not come into use until the early 1800s.

Cheap steel nibs were first made in the 1820s, and in 1884 Lewis Waterman made a fountain pen which could be filled with an eye dropper. Pens which could be filled automatically appeared in the early 1900s. The ballpoint (which needs a sticky ink) was first tried in the 1880s, but did not become a success until the 1940s.

Writing Machines

Henry Mill designed a "writing machine" in 1714. But no-one really wanted such a machine. Secretaries took down letters in shorthand, known since Roman times, and copied them out in "copperplate" handwriting.

The first typewriters were in fact designed during the 1800s as reading aids for the blind. Three Americans – Carlos Glidden, Samuel Soulé and Christopher Sholes – pioneered the typewriter as a writing machine for business use. When the new machine finally became popular in the 1880s, it created many new jobs for working women in the business world.

Counting and Measuring

When man became a farmer, he was able to trade. And he had to learn to count. He counted on his fingers, in tens, and to help with difficult sums he used rows of pebbles in the sand. This idea led to the abacus, the oldest form of calculator, which uses beads threaded on wires.

The First Mathematicians

Priests in ancient Babylon and Egypt studied the moon and stars in order to draw up calendars. These astronomer-priests could predict eclipses. In Egypt they warned farmers when the Nile was about to flood.

The Egyptians used geometry when building the Pyramids. The great mathematicians of Greece, who included Euclid and Pythagoras, made many important discoveries. Another Greek, Ptolemy, drew the first accurate maps of the known world. He was also an astronomer and his idea that the sun and planets circled the Earth was accepted for over a thousand years.

The Growth of Science

In the 1500s two great astronomers, Copernicus and Kepler, who used the records of Tycho Brahe, challenged Ptolemy's ideas. They proved that in

Cubit rule

Meter rule

▲ This portrait (c. 1506) of the Italian mathematician-monk Fra Luca di Pacioli, who wrote a 600-page book on arithmetic and geometry, shows him demonstrating a theorem.

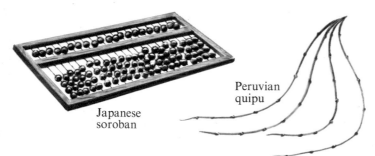

Japanese soroban

Peruvian quipu

Pocket calculator

At first people measured distance with rods and knotted cords. Weights and volumes were based on the different containers used for holding wine and grain. Units of measurement were often based on the human body, and there were many different ones. The metric system was an attempt to standardise weights and measures. A metre was originally one ten-millionth of the distance from the North Pole to the Equator.

The abacus has been used since ancient times. Its modern counterpart is the far more sophisticated electronic pocket calculator.

Babylonian log

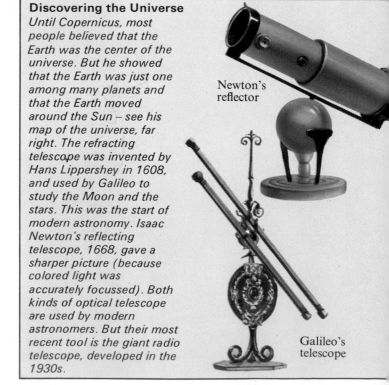

Newton's reflector

Galileo's telescope

Discovering the Universe
Until Copernicus, most people believed that the Earth was the center of the universe. But he showed that the Earth was just one among many planets and that the Earth moved around the Sun – see his map of the universe, far right. The refracting telescope was invented by Hans Lippershey in 1608, and used by Galileo to study the Moon and the stars. This was the start of modern astronomy. Isaac Newton's reflecting telescope, 1668, gave a sharper picture (because colored light was accurately focussed). Both kinds of optical telescope are used by modern astronomers. But their most recent tool is the giant radio telescope, developed in the 1930s.

fact the Earth and the other planets circle the sun.

As science developed, new instruments were needed to measure the natural world. Among them were the thermometer (1593) to measure temperature and the barometer (1643) to measure air pressure. Later came the galvanometer (1832) which measures electrical current, and the Geiger counter (1910) for measuring radioactivity.

Counting Faster

Two useful early aids to mathematics were logarithms (invented in 1614) and the slide rule (1621). Blaise Pascal's calculating machine of 1642 was ahead of its time. Electronic computers did not appear until 1946.

Computers count using only two symbols, 0 and 1. This "binary code" was first described in 1679 by Leibnitz. The numerals we use today came originally from India. They reached Europe, by way of the Arabs, around 1000 AD.

The first units of measurement were based on the human body. A cubit was the distance from elbow to finger tip. An acre was the amount of land a man could plow in a day. There were many different weights and measures. The yard was originally defined in the 12th century as the distance from the nose of King Henry I of England to his fingertips. In 1791 France adopted a simplified metric system which is now used all over the world.

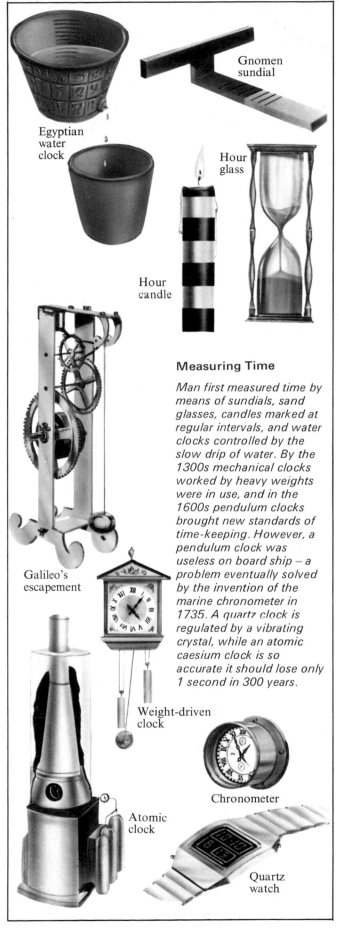

Gnomen sundial

Egyptian water clock

Hour glass

Hour candle

Measuring Time

Man first measured time by means of sundials, sand glasses, candles marked at regular intervals, and water clocks controlled by the slow drip of water. By the 1300s mechanical clocks worked by heavy weights were in use, and in the 1600s pendulum clocks brought new standards of time-keeping. However, a pendulum clock was useless on board ship – a problem eventually solved by the invention of the marine chronometer in 1735. A quartz clock is regulated by a vibrating crystal, while an atomic caesium clock is so accurate it should lose only 1 second in 300 years.

Galileo's escapement

Weight-driven clock

Atomic clock

Chronometer

Quartz watch

◀ *A woodcut printed by Caxton in the 1480s. A picture was cut into a wooden block, inked and then hand-stamped onto the paper.*

▲ *In modern lithography, the printing surface or plates – often prepared photographically – are fitted around a cylinder in a high-speed rotary press.*

Books and Printing

Among the first books were the histories of ancient Egypt, written on papyrus scrolls. Papyrus was a kind of paper made from strips of reed soaked in water and pasted together into a sheet.

A long scroll, rolled on two sticks, was awkward to carry around. So for everyday use people wrote on small tablets of wood or wax. The first books, as we know them, were made in Roman times. The Romans wrote on sheets of parchment, a very thin leather, and bound several pages together inside a protective cover, to make a book.

Making Books by Hand

During the Middle Ages most books were copied out and illustrated by hand. This laborious work was done by monks, for few ordinary people could read and write. Books were large, and so precious they were often kept chained up.

The Chinese had discovered how to print on paper, using a wooden block with characters or letters cut into its surface. Woodcuts were known in Europe, but this form of printing was very slow.

Paper and Printing

In the 8th century the Arabs captured some Chinese paper-makers and learnt the secret of making paper from rags. Paper-making reached Europe, and a cheaper, faster way of making books was at hand.

The breakthrough came in Germany in the 1400s. Johann Gutenberg built a printing press with metal "type" (letters) which could be arranged in any order. This invention had an enormous impact on the spread of knowledge. In the following years presses were improved and methods of engraving and etching pictures developed. From the 1520s newspapers began to appear in Europe.

Modern Printing

Modern printing dates from the invention of lithography (fast picture-printing) by Aloys Senefelder in 1798 and the introduction of steam-powered presses in the 1800s. Type had to be arranged or "composed" by hand until the invention of automatic type-casting machines. With the Linotype machine (1886) type could be cast as it was needed and melted down after use.

Today books, magazines and newspapers are part of our daily lives. High-speed machinery, using photographic techniques and computers, print the millions of words in dozens of languages which are read every day, including the book you are reading now.

Paper making in the 17th century.

1.Wheel-driven trip hammers, fitted with spikes, shred rags mixed with water to a pulp. 2.The pulp was transferred to a vat and stirred. Then a wire screen or sieve was dipped into the pulp, lifted out, shaken and laid on a piece of felt. The paper then stuck to the felt. 3.The wet sheets were screw-pressed to squeeze out the moisture and compress the fibres. 4.The finished paper was peeled from the felt and hung to dry.

▼ *Printing in the 1500s. The man composing (setting) the type picks out letters and arranges them in a composing stick held in his left hand. The lines of type are arranged in a tray and inked. To check that no mistakes have been made, a "galley proof" is taken before the type is tapped firmly into the forme ready for printing. The screw press itself is hand operated and after being printed, the wet sheets are hung up to dry.*

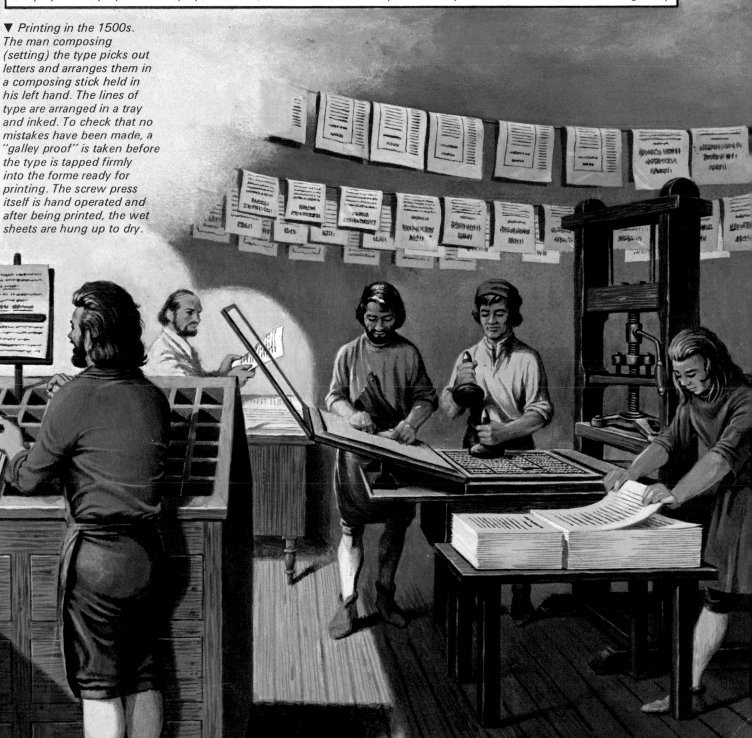

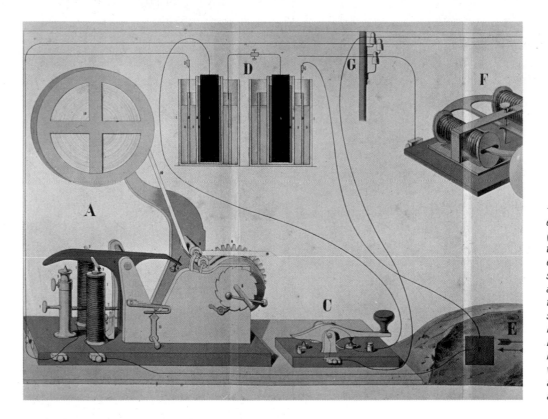

◀ A diagram of Morse's electric telegraph system (1882). From the 1770s there were many experiments with telegraph systems. In 1839 Cooke and Wheatstone installed the first commercially successful telegraph line in England. But Morse invented a code to translate messages over the wires which was simple to use and so his method was adopted.

Messages through the Air

In ancient times people sent messages by means of drums, beacon fires or runners. Later, letters were carried by horsemen or in stage coaches. In the 1840s came the first cheap postal services, carried on the new railroads. Ships used signal flags or mirrors which reflected the sun's rays, and special codes were invented for sending messages in this way.

In 1791 Claude Chappé invented the semaphore, a kind of mechanical "arm waver". Semaphores could send messages from hilltop to hilltop far faster than a horse could gallop.

Talking Wires

But even this was not fast enough for governments, businessmen and the railroad companies themselves who needed to send urgent messages ahead of trains. The solution was the electric telegraph, which came into use in 1838. A signal could be sent by passing an electric current along a wire connected to a receiver which clicked each time the current was switched on or off. Samuel Morse invented a telegraph code, replacing the letters of the alphabet with dots and dashes. Before long

telegraph wires were spanning the continents.

The next step was to transmit speech along the wire. Alexander Graham Bell proved that sound waves made by a voice could be changed into electric current, sent along a wire, and then changed back into sounds. He demonstrated the first telephone in 1876. It was an instant success. For the first time people could talk to someone who was far beyond earshot.

The Coming of Radio

Was it possible to send sound messages without wires? James Clerk Maxwell and, later, Heinrich Hertz had shown that it was possible to produce electromagnetic waves or "radiation". These waves traveled at the speed of light. Several engineers wondered if these "Hertzian waves" could be made to carry sounds.

The pioneer of radio was the Italian Guglielmo Marconi. Marconi had his first success in 1895, and in 1901 he sent the first wireless telegraphy message – the Morse code for the letter S – across the Atlantic. Ships fitted the new system, and soon radio telephony made it possible to transmit voices and even music.

The impact of radio was enormous. News could be flashed around the world in minutes. And a new form of entertainment began in the 1920s with the first radio broadcast.

Modern
Transistor

▲ An early Marconi radio
set, with speaker and
headphones. In a modern
radio, the glass tubes have
been replaced by tiny
transistors.

▼ Radio waves can only
travel in straight lines. For
round-the-world
communications, signals are
bounced off orbiting space
satellites and picked up by
dish antennae on the ground.

Videophone,
1970

Bell's first receiver, 1875

Ericsson's magneto
phone, 1892

*Several inventors, including
Edison and Berliner, helped
improve the telephone after
Bell's first telephone
message in 1875. London's
first telephone exchange
opened in 1879, and as the
telephone service
developed, the instrument
itself took on a shape more
familiar to modern eyes.
Bell himself made the first
call on the new New York-
Chicago line in 1892 (top)
and by 1923 it was possible
to speak from London to
New York. The latest
development is the Video-
phone, which allows callers
to see as well as hear one
another.*

◄ An Australian aborigine playing a 'didgeridoo'. This is a primitive wind instrument very like those used by early Stone Age musicians. It is made from a piece of bamboo or from a tree stem hollowed out by termites.

▼ An Italian musician of the Renaissance period. The lute (which was invented in the Middle East) was the 'basic' stringed instrument, which was developed into the lyre, the mandolin, the guitar and (eventually) the violin and other bowed instruments.

Music and Sound Recording

Sounds play an important part in communications. In fact, one of the first message-sending devices was the "talking drum". The first drums were made from hollow logs or clay pots covered with skin. Other ancient musical instruments are bells, reed pipes and horns. The oldest stringed instrument is the lyre or harp, which is more than 4000 years old.

In the early Middle Ages a monk called Guido D'Arezzo wrote down musical notes in the form we use today. As music developed, new instruments were invented. The violin first appeared in the 1500s and was improved by Amati and Stradivarius. The piano was invented in 1709 and reached its modern form in the 1850s.

Music Machines

In 1953 engineers built the first electronic music synthesizer. This machine can analyze and imitate any instrument, and make new sounds of its own. "Radiophonic" music is now part of the electronic age. Earlier musical machines were the musical box, the barrel organ and the pianola. But there was no way of recording sounds until Edison invented the Phonograph in 1877.

Sound Recording

At first Edison experimented with a machine that could convert into sounds the dots and dashes of Morse code and mark the sounds on oiled paper. Later, inspired by the telephone invented in 1876, he found that sounds could be changed into grooves cut by a needle into tin foil. By repeating the process with a second needle and an earpiece, the grooves "played back" the sounds. This machine gave a very distorted sound. But, together with Bell, Edison produced an improved model, the "graphophone" in 1885 in which sound impressions were cut by a needle on a wax cylinder.

The flat disks we know today were first made by Emile Berliner, the inventor of the gramophone,

▲ *A tape recorder dating from the 1930s.*

◄ *Edison first cut a "record" in tinfoil using a metal stylus, and then used a second stylus to reproduce the sound. His first recording was a squeaky version of "Mary had a little lamb". All records were cylindrical until 1887, when Émile Berliner invented the familiar disk record.*

▼ *This modern recording studio contains a wide range of advanced equipment. There are four tape machines and sounds can be modified or backed with other instruments and echo devices.*

and were introduced successfully in the 1890s. By this time, both hand- and electrically-driven gramophones were on sale. Berliner's work and that of Edison had a great effect on cinema as well. Although sound films did not appear until the 1920s, the idea was thought of as early as 1887.

In the early 1930s juke boxes were playing the latest sounds and in 1948 the long-playing record was invented. It had more grooves, turned more slowly, and played for longer.

Tape-Recording

The best way to record sound is to let the vibrations trace patterns on a magnetic tape. This system is used to make modern records, and was invented by Valdemar Poulsen in 1898. Using a small cassette recorder, anyone can now tape and play the sound of his own voice – a feat which would have seemed magical 100 years ago.

The Picture Revolution

Before the invention of photography, people had seen themselves only in mirrors or in paintings. The forerunner of the camera was the "camera obscura", a darkened room or box with a tiny hole to let in light. A glass lens sharpened the image thrown on to a piece of paper, and in the 1600s artists used this simple device to trace objects accurately.

The Birth of Photography

All that was needed for photography was a chemical to "fix" the image. In 1826 J. N. Niepce managed to fix a hazy picture on a light-sensitive asphalt coated plate. In the 1830s his partner, L. J. M. Daguerre, made "positive" pictures using a silver-coated copper plate. The invention which really made photography work was the positive-negative camera of W. H. Fox Talbot (1840).

The Snapshot Craze

The first cameras had heavy metal plates coated with a wet emulsion. In 1884 George Eastman invented dry plastic film, and in 1888 the Eastman-Kodak company began making cheap easy-to-use box cameras. Soon people everywhere were taking "snaps". Color film was investigated as early as 1861, but only came into use after 1935. And in 1947 "instant" pictures became possible, with Edwin Land's invention of the Polaroid camera.

Moving Pictures

By projecting, or showing, pictures very quickly, one after the other, the figures in them appear to move. Edison's Kinetoscope (1891) was the first moving picture projector, and used celluloid film. In 1896 the Lumière brothers' Cinematograph gave the first public film show, in Paris.

The cinema was immediately popular. The first films were silent, but talking pictures appeared in 1927, and color "movies" in the 1930s. But by then the cinema had a rival – television.

Television Conquers All

John Logie Baird demonstrated a mechanical television system, using rotating disks, in 1926. But the rival electronic system of Marconi-EMI, based on the cathode ray tube (invented in the 1920s by Vladimir Zworykin) was finally chosen. The world's first public television service began in Britain in 1936.

Color television began replacing black-and-white in the 1950s. In 1956 videotape recording gave the viewer an "instant replay", and in 1962 the Telstar communications satellite relayed the first television pictures across the Atlantic. Later satellites such as Early Bird (1965) and Intelsat 4 (1971) made round-the-world television a reality.

◄ The first photographers had to carry enough equipment to fill a handcart. The most bulky objects were the camera itself, the tripod and the wet coated plates on which the exposures were made.

► Today's film-makers make use of very sophisticated equipment and can provide startling effects as this photograph taken from Star Wars shows.

▼ Pathé hand-cranked movie camera c. 1920.

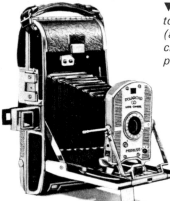

▼ The Lumiere brothers took Edison's Kinetoscope (a kind of peepshow cinema) and added a projector so that films could be shown on a screen. They made their own films to show to audiences in the first cinema show in Paris in 1895.

▲ Chemicals inside the Polaroid camera, invented by Edwin Land in 1947, develop and print the picture in seconds.

▼ Baird's televisor, shown here in its 30-line 1930 version, lost the battle with its rival, the Marconi-EMI electronic television invented by Zworykin. But Baird was the first man to show true television pictures in 1926.

TIME CHART OF INVENTION AND DISCOVERY

Prehistory
Early man-like creatures before 2,000,000 BC. Ice Age begins in northern Europe about 1,000,000 years

First use of tools (pebbles and sticks) * Gradual development of tool-using and tool-making * Hunting and trapping of animals for food * Skins and bones used for clothing and tools * Man learned to make fire about 500,000 years ago

40,000 BC

Emergence of Cro-Magnon man, our direct ancestor * Flint shaped into tools and weapons * Bone needles * Net * Bow and arrow * Cave painting * Bowdrill

10,000 BC
Ice Age ends

Beginnings of village life, in tents and lakeside stilt huts * Clay pots made by hand * Sledge and skiis for transport * Dogs used by hunters * Harpoons, fishing hooks skillfully carved in bone * Oil lamps

7000 BC

Man becomes a farmer, growing crops and keeping animals for food * Copper tools first made * From around 5000 BC mud bricks and the hand loom for weaving cloth come into use * Trade begins

3000 BC
Civilizations of Sumeria, Babylon, Crete, Egypt, China and India

Writing (in Sumeria) * Rope (probably in India) * Irrigation (Egypt) * Wheel (in several places in the Near East) leading to the chariot and the potter's wheel * Plow (hand-pulled), later pulled by animals * Textiles and dyes * Buildings including dams, temples and the Pyramids * Wooden locks * Musical instruments, such as harp and drum * Soap and herbal medicine * 365 day solar calendar in Egypt * Glass-making in Near East

1000 BC
Greek city states. Athens becomes a center of learning. Phoenicians may have sailed round Africa. Alexander the Great reaches India. c. 300 BC Work begins on Great Wall of China. Rise of Rome. Height of Roman Empire AD 100. Rome falls to barbarian invaders, AD 476. 'Dark Ages' in Europe.

Iron gradually replaces bronze for tools and weapons * Papyrus scrolls and wax tablets * Water clocks, sand glasses and sun dials * Umbrella used in China around 1000 BC * Advanced surgery (amputations, cataracts, skin grafts) in India * Kites flown in China * Abacus used in China and Near East * First coins made in Near East around 800 BC * From 600 – 300 BC Greece is the home of brilliant thinkers, inventors and mathematicians (Pythagoras, Archimedes, Euclid, Aristotle and Plato among them) * Alexandria in Egypt has the most famous library and lighthouse in the ancient world * Water wheels, force pumps and simple tools all in use 250 BC * Julian calendar, including leap years, introduced in Rome in 46 BC * Roman builders use cement and concrete * First accurate maps of the known world, such as one drawn by Ptolemy around AD 130 * Paper developed in China around AD 100, known to Arabs by AD 800 and to Europeans by AD 1300 * Windmill invented in Persia and Turkey around AD 600 * Horse collar and stirrups c. AD 800 * Arabic numerals reach Europe c. AD 950 * Vikings almost certainly sailed to North America c. AD 1000

1000 AD
Norman Conquest of England, 1066. First Crusade, 1096. Genghis Khan conquers Asia c. 1200. Marco Polo travels from Italy to China, 1271–95. Black Death in Europe, c. 1350. Renaissance begins in Europe in 1400s. Voyages of discovery to New World and Asia.

Navigation buoys used in Germany (1000) * Gunpowder rocket known in China (1000) * Lateen sail and stern rudder adopted in Europe (by 1200) * Magnetic compass known to Chinese sailors by 1100 and soon afterwards in Europe * Spectacles in use by 1300 * Spinning wheel replaces hand spinning * The longbow and crossbow are effective weapons even against plate armor, which replaces chain mail in the 1300s * First use of cannon in warfare at the Battle of Crecy (1346) * Smock or tower windmills replace earlier postmills * Screw jack (c. 1400) * Printing by movable type, Johann Gutenberg, Germany (1440) * Leonardo da Vinci (b. 1452) makes drawings of human anatomy, designs war machines and a helicopter * Voyages of discovery by Europeans: around the Cape of Good Hope, Bartholomew Diaz, Portugal (1488); to America, Christopher Columbus, Spain (1492); and to India, Vasco da Gama, Portugal (1499)

1500
Reformation in Europe. Spanish conquest of Mexico and Peru. Mogul Empire in India, 1526. Defeat of Spanish Armada, 1588. Shakespeare at work c. 1590–1616.

First circumnavigation of the world, survivors of Magellan's expedition, Portugal (1519–22) * Beginnings of modern anatomy, Andreas Vesalius, Belgium (1514–64) * Theory of solar system, in which the Earth revolves around the Sun, Nicolaus Copernicus, Poland (1543) * Pendulum, Galileo, Italy (1582) * Knitting frame, William Lee, England (1589) * Thermometer (air bulb), Galileo, Italy (1593) * Microscope, Zacharias Janssen, Holland (1590) * New plants (potatoes and tomatoes, for example) brought to Europe from the Americas during the 1500s

1600
Discovery of Australia c. 1605 by the Dutch. Civil war in England, 1642–52. Great Plague, 1665.

Telescope, Hans Lippershey, Holland (1608) * Planetary motion, Johannes Kepler, Germany (1610) * Logarithms, John Napier, Scotland (1614) * Circulation of the blood, William Harvey, England (1619) * Calculator, Blaise Pascal, France (1642) * Barometer, Evangelista Torricelli, Italy (1643) * Pendulum clock, Christiaan Huygens, Holland (1656) * Laws relating gas pressure to volume, Robert Boyle, Ireland (1662) * Reflector telescope, Isaac Newton, England (1669) * Balance spring, Robert Hooke, England (1676) * Binary code, Gottfried Wilhelm von Leibnitz, Germany (1679) * Pressure cooker, Denis Papin, France (1679) * Laws of gravity and motion, Isaac Newton, England (1687) * Steam pump, Thomas Savery, England (1698)

1700
Start of Industrial Revolution in England. Colonization in North America and India. Cook explores Pacific Ocean, Australia and New Zealand. American War of Independence 1775–83. French Revolution 1789.

Iron smelting using coke, Abraham Darby, G.B. (1709) * Mercury thermometer, Gabriel Fahrenheit, Germany (1714) * Improved steam engine, Thomas Newcomen, G.B. (1712) * Sextant, John Hadley, G.B. (1731) * Flying shuttle, John Kay, G.B. (1733) * Chronometer, John Harrison, G.B. (1735) * Celsius or centigrade temperature scale, Anders Celsius, Sweden (1742) * Lightning conductor, Benjamin Franklin, U.S.A. (1752) * Spinning jenny, James Hargreaves, G.B. (1764) * Discovery of hydrogen, Henry Cavendish, G.B. (1766) * Steam carriage, Nicolas Cugnot, France (1769) * Discovery of oxygen, Joseph Priestley, G.B. (1774) * Water closet, Joseph Bramah (a re-invention), G.B. (1778) * Spinning mule, Samuel Crompton, G.B. (1779) * Beginnings of modern surgery, John Hunter, G.B. (1780) * Planet Uranus discovered, William Herschel, G.B. (1781) * Double-acting steam engine, James Watt, G.B. (1782) * Inoculation, Edward Jenner, G.B. (1796)

1800
Napoleonic Wars end in 1815.

Battery, Alessandro Volta, Italy (1800) * Steam locomotive, Richard Trevithick, G.B. (1804) * Steamship, Robert Fulton U.S.A. (1807) * Atomic theory, John Dalton, G.B. (1807) * Food canning, Nicolas Appert, France (1809) * Miners' safety lamp, Humphry Davy, G.B. (1815) * Molecular structure, Amadeo Avogradro, Italy (1811) * Electromagnetism, Hans Christian Oersted, Denmark (1820)

1820 National movements in Europe. Poor emigrants look to the United States for a new life. Abolition of slavery, 1833.	Gas lighting becomes common in city streets * Electric motor, Michael Faraday, G.B. (1821) * Calculating machine, Charles Babbage, G.B. (1823) * Portland cement, Joseph Aspdin, G.B. (1824) * Laws of electromagnetism, André Ampere, France (1826) * Laws of electric conduction, Georg Ohm, Germany (1827) * Friction match, John Walker, G.B. (1827) * Braille alphabet, Louis Braille, France (1829) * Sewing machine, Barthélemy Thimmonier, France (1830) * Dynamo, Michael Faraday, G.B. (1831) * Steam railway, George Stephenson, G.B. (1830) * Reaping machine, Cyrus McCormick, U.S.A. (1834) * Refrigeration, Jacob Perkins, G.B. (1834) * Revolver, Samuel Colt, U.S.A. (1836) * Screw propeller, John Ericsson, Sweden (1836) * Telegraph, Samuel Morse, U.S.A. (1837) * Bicycle, Kirkpatrick Macmillan, G.B. (1839)
1840 Trade Unions develop. Revolutions in Europe. Karl Marx publishes Communist Manifesto, 1848. Crimean War, 1854–56.	Photography, Louis Jacques Daguerre, France and William Fox Talbot, G.B. (1840) * Postage stamp, Rowland Hill, G.B. (1840) * Anesthetics, Crawford Long, U.S.A. (1842) * Vulcanized rubber, Charles Goodyear, U.S.A. (1844) * Discovery of planet Neptune, Johann Galle, Germany (1846) * Automatic lift, Elisha Otis, U.S.A. (1850) * Airship, Henri Giffard, France (1852) * Manned glider, Sir George Cayley, G.B. (1853) * Safety matches, Johan and Carl Lundstrom, Sweden, (1855) * Bessemer steel process, Sir Henry Bessemer, G.B. (1856)
1860 Explorations in Africa by Speke, Livingstone and Stanley. U.S. Civil War, 1861–65. Suez Canal opened, 1869. Japan begins to adopt western ideas.	Can opener, inventor unknown, some time after 1860 * Underground railroad, Charles Pearson, G.B. (1863) * Pasteurization, Louis Pasteur, France (1863) * Light radiation theory, James Clerk Maxwell, G.B. (1864) * Antiseptic surgery, Joseph Lister, G.B. (1865) * Laws of inheritance, Gregor Mendel, Austria (1866) * Dynamite, Alfred Nobel, Sweden (1866) * Lawn mower, Amariah Hills, U.S.A. (1868) * Celluloid (first plastic), J. W. Hyatt, U.S.A. (1868) * Margarine, Hippolyte Mège-Mouriéz, France (1870) * Barbed wire, Joseph Glidden, U.S.A. (1873) * Typewriter, Christopher L. Sholes, U.S.A. (1873) * Internal combustion engine, Nikolaus Otto, Germany (1876) * Telephone, A. G. Bell, U.S.A. (1876) * Phonograph, Thomas Edison, U.S.A. (1877) * Incandescent light bulb, Joseph Swan, G.B. (1878) and Edison (1879)
1880 British Empire at its height. Russia, Austria-Hungary and China are in decline. Nansen explores the Arctic. Africa split into colonies by the European countries.	Inoculation, Louis Pasteur, France (1880) * Machine gun, Hiram Maxim, U.S.A. (1884) * Motor car, Karl Benz, Germany (1885) * Linotype printing, Otto Mergenthaler, U.S.A. (1885) * Esperanto (artificial language), Ludwik Zamenhof, Poland (1887) * Radio waves, Heinrich Hertz, Germany (1887) * Combine harvester, in use in U.S.A. (c. 1887) * Roll-film camera, George Eastman, U.S.A. (1888) * Pneumatic tyre, John Dunlop, G.B. (1888) * Rayon developed by French chemists (1890) * Diesel engine, Rudolf Diesel, Germany (1893) * Zip fastener, Whitcomb Judson, U.S.A. (1893) * First cinema shows, Louis and Auguste Lumière, France, (1895) * Radio, Guglielmo Marconi, Italy (1895) * Safety razor, King, C. Gillette, U.S.A. (1895) * X-rays, Willhelm von Roentgen, Germany (1895) * Manned glider experiments by Otto Lilienthal, Germany (1891–96) * Breakfast cereals marketed by Charles Post and the Kellogg brothers, U.S.A. (1890s) * Radium discovered by Marie and Pierre Curie, Poland, 1898 * Tape recorder, Valdemar Poulsen, Denmark (1899)
1900 Russo-Japanese War, 1904–05. China becomes a republic, 1911. World War I 1914–18. Russian Revolution, 1917.	First trans-Atlantic radio signals, Guglielmo Marconi, Italy (1901) * Vacuum cleaner Hubert Booth, G.B. (1901) * First airplane flight, Orville Wright, U.S.A. (1903) * Hydrofoil, Enrico Forlanini, Italy (1905) * Special theory of relativity (i.e. all motion is relative), Albert Einstein, Germany (1905) * Helicopter (not developed), Paul Cornu, France (1907) * First cheap family car, the Model T, Henry Ford, U.S.A. (1908) * Electric washing machine, Alva Fisher, U.S.A. (1910) * Geiger counter, Hans Geiger, Germany (1910) * Model of the atom, Ernest Rutherford, New Zealand and Niels Bohr, Denmark (1911) * Conveyor belt to speed up factory production, Henry Ford, U.S.A. (1913) * General theory of relativity (laws affecting light, gravity and energy), Albert Einstein, Germany (1915) * Soapless detergents (1916)
1920 Stalin succeeds Lenin as ruler of Soviet Union, 1924. World trade slumps and many people are without jobs. Hitler rises to power in Germany. Radio and the cinema very popular.	Quick-frozen food, Clarence Birdseye, U.S.A. (1925) * Television (mechanical system), John Logie Baird, G.B. (1926) * Liquid-fueled rocket, Robert Goddard, U.S.A. (1926) * Penicillin isolated by Alexander Fleming, G.B. (1928) * Electronic television system (using cathode ray tube receiver), Vladimir Zworykin, U.S.A. (1929) * Heart/lung machine, Philip Drinker, U.S.A. (1929) * Planet Pluto discovered, Clyde Tombaugh, U.S.A. (1930) * First patent for a jet engine, Frank Whittle, G.B. (1930) * Radio telescope, Karl Jansky, U.S.A. (1931) * Electron microscope, suggested by Louis de Broglie, France, developed by Rudenberg, Knoll, Ruska and Zworykin, U.S.A. (1931) * Radar, Robert Watson-Watt, G.B. (c. 1935) * First practical helicopter, Focke-Achgelis FW–61, Germany (1936) * Nylon, Wallace Carothers, U.S.A. (1936) * First public television service by B.B.C., G.B. (1936) * Ballpoint pen, Ladislao and Georg Biro, Hungary (1938) * Antibiotic (penicillin), Howard Florey, Australia and Ernst Chain, G.B. (1938) * Jet aircraft, (Heinkel 178), Germany (1939)
1940 World War II, 1939–45. United Nations founded 1945. Communists take over in China 1949. 'Cold War' between USSR and USA. Korean War, 1950–53. Most former colonies in Africa and Asia become independent by 1960s.	Xerox photocopier, Chester Carlson, U.S.A. (1940) * Aerosol, Lyle Goodhue, U.S.A. (1941) * Nuclear reactor, Enrico Fermi, Italy and others (in the U.S.A.), (1942) * Kidney machine, William Kolff, Holland (1944) * Guided missile (V2), Wernher von Braun, Germany (1944) * Atomic bomb, team of U.S., British, and Canadian scientists led by Robert Oppenheimer (1945) * Computer, J. P. Eckert and J. W. Mauchly, U.S.A. (1946) * Polaroid camera, Edwin Land, U.S.A. (1947) * First supersonic level flight by a manned aircraft, Bell XS–1, U.S.A. (1947) * Transistor, William Shockley, John Bardeen and Walter Brattain, U.S.A. (1948) * Long playing records introduced in U.S.A. (1948) * Holography (three-dimensional photography) suggested by Denis Gabor, Hungary (1949) * Hydrogen bomb, first test explosion by U.S.A. (1952) * Contraceptive pill, a new means of birth control for women, developed by Gregory Pincus and others, U.S.A. (1955) * Rotary engine for cars, Felix Wankel, Germany (1956) * First practical nuclear power station, Calder Hall, G.B. (1956) * Videotape recording, A. Poniatoff, U.S.A. (1956) * First artificial Earth satellite, Sputnik, U.S.S.R. (1957) * Fuel cell, Francis Bacon, G.B. (1959) * Hovercraft (SR–N1), Christopher Cockerell, G.B. (1959)
1960 Wars in Vietnam and the Middle East. Concern about pollution and the energy crisis. Widening gap between rich industrial nations and the developing countries of the Third World. Greater freedom for women in the West.	Laser, Theodore Maiman, U.S.A. (1960) * First manned spaceflight, Yuri Gagarin, U.S.S.R. (1961) * First Communications satellite for relaying telephone and television signals (Telstar), U.S.A. (1962) * Quasars (quasi-stellar radio source), the furthest and brightest objects observed from Earth, discovered by Thomas Matthews and Allan Sandage, U.S.A. (1963) * First heart transplant operation on a human patient, Christian Barnard, South Africa (1967) * First Moon landing by Apollo 11 astronauts Neil Armstrong and Edwin Aldrin, U.S.A. (1969) * Concorde supersonic airliner enters regular airline service, G.B. and France (1976) * First controlled soft-landings of unmanned spacecraft (Vikings) on Mars, U.S.A. (1976)

Fact Index

Most of the entries in this Fact Index are followed by one or more page numbers. These refer you to pages in the book where there is an article or information on that entry. Some of the entries followed by page numbers themselves contain information. A few entries give information only, and are not followed by page numbers. Page numbers in **bold** type indicate illustrations.

A

Abacus 78
Acupuncture 52, **52**
Adhesives or glues have been in use since ancient times. Egyptian carpenters made glue from animal bones. Synthetic adhesives were invented in the 1930s.
Aerosol. A pressurized container filled with a mixture of gas and other substances, such as paint or hair spray; it was invented in 1941 by the American scientist Lyle David Goodhue.

▲ Abacus, 500 BC

Aircraft 66, 67
Airport 66
Airship 66, **67**
Alchemy is the mixture of science and magic practised in the Middle Ages. 30, 52
Alphabet 76
Aluminum 31
Ammunition 72
Anatomy 52, **54**
Anesthetics 54, 55
Antibiotics 54
Antiseptics 54
Aqualung or scuba ('self-contained underwater breathing apparatus') was developed in the 1940s by Jacques-Yves Cousteau (France) and others.
Aqueduct 35, 37

Arch 35, **36**
Archimedes (287–212 BC) Greek mathematician 20; Archimedes's screw **21**
Arkwright, Richard (1732–1792) English inventor of spinning machinery 27
Armor 70, **71**
Artificial diamonds were first made for industrial use, in the USA (1955).
Artificial limbs were pioneered in the 1500s by Ambroise Paré. **53**
Artificial satellite 67, **83**, 86
Aspirin was first used as a pain-killer in the 1890s.
Assembly line 31, **31**
Assyria 70; archers **70**
Astrolabe. Known in Greece in the first century BC, this navigational instrument was used by sailors to measure the positions of stars. It was later replaced by the sextant.
Astronomy 78, **78**
Atomic structure. An early theory was that of Democritus (400 BC). Later theories were put forward by John Dalton (GB) in 1807 and Amadeo Avogadro (Italy) in 1811. Modern ideas about the atom are based on the work of Rutherford and Bohr in the early 1900s. 20
Automation 31, **31**

B

Backstaff 64
Bacteria 54
Baird, John Logie (1888–1946) Scottish television pioneer 86
Balance 20
Ballista 70
Balloon 66, **66**
Ball bearings were first made in the 1790s but not widely used until the 1860s when the bicycle became popular. Leonardo da Vinci drew designs for roller bearings in the late 1400s.
Ballpoint pen 77, **77**
Barbed wire was invented in 1873 by Joseph Glidden (USA). It was immediately popular with farmers.
Barometer 79
Bath 46, **47**
Bathyscaphe, a deep sea diving vessel first used in 1948.
Battery 28, 29
Bell, Alexander Graham (1847–1922) US inventor 82, **83**
Bellows 17, 18, **19**
Benz, Karl Friedrich (1844–1929) German engineer 60

Bessemer converter 30
Bicycle 60, **61**
Binary code 79
Blood circulation 52
Blood transfusions, using animal donors were tried in the 1700s, but the modern technique was first used in 1818.
Boat 64
Bolas were throwing weapons consisting of weighted cords which tangled up the legs of the prey. 12
Bomb 72; atomic bomb 69, 72, **72**
Book 74, 80
Boring mill 27
Bow and arrow 12, **70**
Bowdrill, **12**, **19**, 21
Brahe, Tycho (1546–1601) Danish astronomer 78
Braille 76
Breakfast foods were first produced by Charles Post and John and Will Keith Kellogg in the 1890s.
Bricks 34, **34**, 36, **36**
Bridge 37, **37**, **38**
Bronze 16, 18
Brunel, Sir Marc Isambard (1769–1849) French-born engineer 38; his son Isambard Kingdom Brunel (1806–1859) built bridges, railways and the largest steamships of the day.
Building 16, **18**, 32–39
Bulldozer 36
Buoy 64
Buttons 48

C

Calculator 78, 79
Calendar 75, 78
Camera 86, **86**, **87**
Canal 36, **37**
Candle 45, **79**
Cannon 72, **73**
Canoe 12, 64, **65**
Can opener 44
Carburetors were invented in the 1890s and were essential to the development of gasoline-driven motor vehicles.
Carpentry 14, **19**
Carpet sweeper 46
Cartwright, Edmund (1743–1823) English inventor of the power loom 27
Casting metal 16, **16**
Cast iron 28; bridge 37
Castle 70, **71**
Caterpillar tracks were invented in 1904 and used first on tanks and later on tractors and bulldozers.
Cathode ray tube 86
Catseye 61
Cave-dwellers 10–11, 12
Cave painting 8
Cayley, Sir George (1773–1857) English glider pioneer 66
Cement 38, **38**

Central heating 46
Chain 61
Charcoal 18
Chariot 58
Chess 49
Chimneys began to be built in European houses from the 1500s. 46
China: alphabet 76; gunpowder 72; medicine 52; paper and printing 80
Chronometer 64, **79**
Cigarettes were originally a cheap form of the cigar, which was introduced to Europe around 1600. They became widely popular after 1870.
Cinema 86, **87**
Clocks 79
Clothing 10, 48
Coins, 17, **17**
Coke 28
Color film 86
Column 36, **36**

▲ Electronic Computer, 1946

Combine harvester 43
Communications 74–87
Compass 64, **64**
Computer 31
Concorde 67
Contraceptive pills were developed by Dr Gregory Pincus and others in the United States in the 1950s.
Cooking 10, 44; kitchen range **41**
Copernicus, Nicolaus (1473–1543) Polish astronomer 78
Copper 15, 16
Corrugated iron sheets were first used to roof buildings in the 1820s.
Cosmetics were probably first used in China but the earliest record of their use comes from Egypt around 3750 BC.
Cotton gin (1793). A machine invented by Eli Whitney (USA), to separate the seeds from cotton fibers mechanically.
Crane 33, 35
Crankshaft 27
Cro-Magnon man 12
Crop rotation 42
Crossbow 70
Cugnot, Nicolas (1725–1804) French engineer who

The Elements

It was once thought that the world was made up of four elements – earth, air, fire and water. In fact there are at least 107 elements. In 1661 Robert Boyle suggested that an element was a substance (like iron) which cannot be split into smaller substances. Some elements have been known since ancient times. Others were discovered by alchemists, or by early chemists who discovered the most important gases making up the air (hydrogen, 1766; nitrogen, 1772; and oxygen, 1774). Humphry Davy proved that electrolysis was one way of splitting up a substance into its various elements. And in the past 150 years many more elements have been discovered. In the 1800s a Russian chemist called Mendeleyev predicted the existence of most of these elements before they had in fact been discovered. Most elements are named after the person who discovered them or the place where they were found. Some are very rare and can only be made in laboratories by bombarding uranium atoms with neutrons.

built the first powered vehicle. 58, **59**
Cuneiform writing 76, **76**
Cyclotron or particle accelerator. Invented in 1833 by Ernest Lawrence and Milton Livingstone (USA), this machine bombards elements to break down their atomic structure and change them into different substances.

D
Daimler, Gottlieb (1834–1900) German engineer 60
Dam 42. Early dams (from around 2500 BC) were used to store irrigation water. Damming rivers for hydroelectric power began in the 1900s.
Darby, Abraham (1677–1717) English industrialist 28
DDT (dichloro-diphenyl-trichloroethane), insecticide first made in Switzerland (1939). 43
Dentistry 55
Detergents 46
Diesel, Rudolf (1858–1913) German engineer 61
Diesel locomotive 63
Diode Electronic radio valve; it was invented in 1904 by Sir Ambrose Fleming (GB).
Diving suit. The first practical diving suit was made in 1830 by Augustus Siebe (Germany).
Dome 36
Domestic animals 12, 24, 42
Drains 39, 54
Dredgers were first used to clear canals in Holland in the 1400s.
Drugs 54
Dyes 16, 17
Dynamite 38
Dynamo 28, 29

E
Edison, Thomas Alva (1847–1931) US inventor 45, 84, 86
Egypt 88; astronomy 78; building 34; farming 42, **42**; papyrus **77**, 80; warfare 70
Einstein, Albert (1879–1955) German-born mathematician and physicist 89
Elastic 30
Electric blankets were first tried in the early 1900s and became popular after the 1930s.
Electricity 25, 29, 45; electric car 60; electric motor 29; electric railway 62
Electromagnetism 29
Electronics 30, 31; computer 79; music 84; television 87; transistor **83**
Electron microscope. Invented in the 1930s, it uses an electron beam instead of light rays.
Elevator 35, **35**, **38**
Enclosure of fields 42
Entertainment 49
Esperanto, an artificial language invented by Dr L. Zamenhof (Russia) in 1887.
Excavator 36, **37**
Explosives 38, 72, **72**

F
Factory 27, **31**
False teeth were first used around 500 BC. Poor people sold their teeth to be transplanted into the mouths of rich people, before the invention of porcelain and plastic dentures.
Faraday, Michael (1791–1867) English physicist 29
Farming 12, 24, 42–43
Fermi, Enrico (1901–1954) Italian physicist who led the scientists responsible for the world's first nuclear reactor. 30
Fertilizer 43

Feudal system 70; strip farming 42
Film, photographic 86
Fire-making 10, 12, **12**
Fishing 12, **13**
Fleming, Sir Alexander (1881–1955) Scottish discoverer of penicillin 54
Flintlock musket 73
Flint tools 10, **10**, 12, **12**
Fluorescent lamp 45
Food 42, 43; cooking 44; preservation 44
Foot rule 78
Ford, Henry (1863–1947) US industrialist 31
Fountain pen 77, **77**
Franklin, Benjamin (1706–1790) US statesman, writer and inventor 28, **29**
Freud, Sigmund (1856–1939) Austrian psychologist 55
Frozen foods were first sold successfully in the USA by Clarence Birdseye in the 1930s. 44
Fuel cell. A source of electric power using hydrogen and oxygen as fuel; it was invented in 1960 by Francis Bacon (GB).

G
Galen (c. 130–200) Greek physician 52
Galilei, Galileo (1564–1642) Italian astronomer who made a barometer, telescope and a thermoscope. **53, 78**
Galvani, Luigi (1737–1798) Italian scientist who stumbled on the principle of the wet battery by accident. 29
Galvanometer 79
Games 49
Gas 28, 30; heating 46, **47**; lighting 45, **45**
Gas mask 73
Gears 21, 24; 'sun and planet' gearing **26**, 27
Geiger counter 79
Generator 25, **28**, 29
Geometry 78
Germs 54
Glass 17, 18
Glider 57, 66

▲ Gunpowder, AD 1000

Gramophone 84
Greece 88; clothing 48; games 49; mathematics 78; medicine 52; phalanx 70
Guericke, Otto von (1602–1686) German mathematician 27
Guided missile 72, **73**
Gunpowder 72, **72**
Gyroscope. Invented in 1852, the gyroscope is now used in gyrocompasses on board ships and aircraft.

H
Hand ax 10
Hargreaves, James (c. 1720–1778) English inventor of the spinning jenny 27
Harp 84
Harvey, William (1578–1657) English physician 52
Hearing aids were at first trumpet-shaped horns. The electronic hearing aid was invented by Edwin Stevens (USA) in 1935.
Heart-lung machine 55
Heating (domestic) 46, **47**
Helicopter 66, 67
Heredity. The science of genetics and heredity began with the work of the Austrian monk Gregor Mendel (1822–1884).
Hertz, Heinrich (1857–1894) German physicist 82
Hieroglyphics 76
Hippocrates (c. 460–377 BC) Greek physician 52
Holography. The theory of holography (the reconstruction of an object as a three dimensional image) was first described by Dennis Gabor in 1948. Since the invention of the laser in 1960 the creation of holograms has become possible.
Horse 58, **58**, 70
Hourglass 79, **79**
Hovercraft 64, **65**
Hunting 10, 12
Hydro-electric power 25
Hydrofoil 64
Hygiene 39, 41, 54
Hypocaust 46

I
Icecream 44
Inclined plane 20, **21**, 34, **37**
Incubator 55
India 46, 48; chess 49; warfare **68**
Industrial Revolution 27, 41, 48, 62
Ink 76, **76**, 77
Insecticide 43
Internal combustion engine 59, 60
Interior decoration 39
Irrigation 24, **42**
Iron 18; cast iron bridge 37; smelting 28; smith 18, **19**

J

Jenner, Edward (1749–1823) English country doctor who experimented with vaccination. 54
Jet engine 67
Juke box 85

K

Kepler, Johannes (1571–1630) German astronomer 78
Kidney machine 55
Knitting frame. Invented in 1596 by an English clergyman, William Lee.

L

Lancet 53
Language laboratory 77
Laser. An instrument which produces pure light. Ordinary light is made up of waves of different lengths. But laser light is composed of waves of identical length. It was first produced by Theodore H. Maiman in 1960. **4–5**

▲ Laser, 1960

Lathe 16, **19**, 27
Lawn mowers were first invented in 1805 and then improved by Edwin Budding in 1830.
Leibnitz, Gottfried Wilhelm von (1646–1716) German mathematician 79
Leonardo da Vinci (1452–1519) Italian scientist, artist and writer 20, 52, **66**
Lever 20, 21, **21**
Light bulb 45, **45**
Lighthouse 64
Lighting 45, **45**
Lilienthal, Otto (1848–1896) German aviation pioneer **57**, 66
Linotype printing 80
Lister, Joseph (1827–1912) Scottish surgeon 53, 54
Lithography 80, **80**
Locks and keys 18
Logarithms 79
Long-playing record 85
Loom 16, 17, 27, **27**

M

Machine gun 73
Machines, simple 15, 20, **21**
Machine tools 30

Magic 52
Magic lantern. Invented in 1875 by J.A.R. Rudge for showing slides.
Magnetism has been known since ancient times in the 'lodestone'; compass 64, **64**; electromagnetism 29; magnetic tape recording 85
Map 78, 79
Marconi, Guglielmo (1874–1937) Italian-born pioneer of radio 82

▼ Safety Match, 1840s

Margarine. One of the first man-made foods, it was invented by Hippolyte Mège Mouriéz in 1869.
Matches 12, **45**
Matchlock musket 73
Mathematics 78
Maxwell, James Clerk (1831–1879) Scottish physicist 82
Measurement 78–79
Medicine 50–55
Mesopotamia 12, 17, 34, 42
Metal-working 15, **16**, 17, **19**; iron 18; steel 31
Metric system 79
Microscope 51, **51**, **53**, 54
Microwave oven 45
Miners' safety lamp. Invented by Humphry Davy in 1815, this lamp lessened the risk of explosions in mines.
Mining 12, 28
Moon landing 67
Money 16, 17; paper money was invented in China before AD 800, but was slow to catch on in Europe.
Montgolfier, Joseph (1740–1810) and Etienne (1745–1799) French balloon pioneers 66
Morse, Samuel (1791–1872) US inventor 82
Motor car 31, **56**, 57, 58–61
Motor cycle 60, **61**
Motorway 61
Music 84
Musket 68, 72, **73**

N

Nail 31, 36
Natural gas 30
Neanderthal man 12
Needle 10, 18
Net 13
Newspaper 80
Newton, Sir Isaac (1642–1727) English scientist who described the laws of motion and built the first reflecting telescope. 78
Non-stick pan 45
Nuclear energy 29, 30
Nylon 48

O

Oersted, Hans Christian (1777–1851) Danish physicist 29
Oil 28, 30; oil lamp 30, 45, **45** oil heating 46
Opthalmoscope 53
Oxen 42, 58

P

Paddle steamer 64, **65**
Paper 77, 80, 81
Papyrus 80
Parachute jumping was demonstrated by Jacques Garnerin (France) in 1797. Leonardo sketched a parachute design in 1485.
Paraffin 45
Parking meters were first used in the 1930s in the USA.
Pascal, Blaise (1623–62) French mathematician 79
Pasteur, Louis (1822–95) French biologist 52, 54; 'pasteurized' milk 54
Pattern (dress-making) 48
Pen 76, **77**
Pencil 77, **77**
Penicillin 54
Phonograph 75, 84, **85**
Photoelectric cells (used in cinema, television and burglar alarms) were first invented and used by the German physicist Arthur Korn in 1902. Today other types of photoelectric cells are in use.
Photography 86, **86**, **87**
Piano 84
Plaster 36
Plastics 30, 31
Playing cards 49
Plough 20, **20**, 42, **42**
Pneumatic drill 37, 38
Polaroid camera 86, 87
Postage stamps were first used in Britain in 1840; they were the idea of Rowland Hill.
Postal services 82
Pottery 12, **15**, 17, **17**
Prefabricated buildings 38
Pressure cooker 45
Printed circuit 30, 31
Printing 75, 80–81
Psychoanalysis 55

▼ Newton's laws of gravity and motion, 1687

Ptolemy (2nd century AD) Greek geographer 78
Pulley 13, 16, 20, **35**
Pump 20, 21, **21**, 27
Pyramids 20, 34, **34**

Q

Quern 9
Quill 74, 77

R

Radar 66, 67
Radiator 47
Radio 82, **83**
Radio telescopes were invented in the 1930s by Karl Jansky (USA) and others.
Raft 64, **65**
Railways 62–63
Razor (safety) 41, **47**
Record player 84
Recording studio 85
Refrigeration 44, **44**
Respirator 53; heart-lung machine 55
Revolver 73
Rifle 72
Road-making 60, **60**
Robot 31
Rocket 67, 72
Roentgen, Wilhelm von (1845–1923) German physicist 55
Romans (ancient): books 80; building 34, 35, **35**, 36, 37, 38; clothing 48; farming 42; stone masons **19**; warfare 70
Rubber reached Europe from Peru in the 1730s. Elastic was invented by Charles Macintosh and Thomas Hancock in the 1820s and 'vulcanized' rubber invented by Charles Goodyear in 1841. **30**, 31

S

Safety pins were invented in the 1840s although pins of similar design have been used since ancient times. 48

▲ Safety pin, 1849

Scaffolding 35, **35**
Screw. The first screws were threaded nails hammered into wood. Screwdrivers were developed from a 'turnscrew' used by 16th century gunsmiths to adjust gun workings. 30
Screw press 21
Screw propeller 64
Semaphore 62, 82
Sewers 38, 39, 46
Sewing machine 48, **48**
Sextant 64
Shaduf 20, **42**
Ships 64–65

Shoes 48
Shorthand writing 77
Shuttle, flying 27
Siege 68, 70, 71
Skyscraper 32, **35**, 39
Sledge 34, 58
Slide rule 79
Soap 46, **46**
Solar furnace 25, **25**
Solar panels 25
Sound recording 84, **85**
Spaceflight 67
Spear 12, 69, **70** halberd 70
Spectacles 53, **53**, **74**
Spin drier 46
Spinning 16, 17, **26**, 27
Steam carriages 58
Steam engine 23, **26**, 27; steam cars 60; railroads **62**; ship 64, **65**

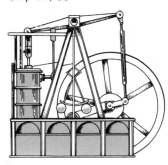

▲ Steam Engine, 1700s

Steel 18, **31**, 38; steel mill 30, **31**
Stephenson, George (1781–1848) English railroad engineer 62
Stethoscope 53, 55
Stirrups 58, 70
Stone Age 10, **10–11**; farming 42
Street lighting 45
Strip farming 42
Submarine. After the experiments of Bushnell and others, the first pratical submarines were the diesel-electric boats of US designer John P. Holland (1890s). 65, **65**
Sundial 79
Surgery 50, 52, 55
Swan, Sir Joseph (1828–1914) English scientist 45
Sword 18
Synthesizer 84

T
Tank 72, **73**
Tape recorder 85, **85**
Telegraph 82, **82**
Telephone 82, **83**
Telescope 78, **78**
Television 86, **87**
Tent 34, **34**
Textiles 48; textile industry 27
Thermometer 53, 79
Threshing 42
Tidal power 25
Tinderbox 12, 45

▲ Radio, 1895; Television, 1920s

Tools 9, 10, 14–21; machine tools 21, 30
Torpedoes were developed by Robert Whitehead (GB), 1866. 72
Town planning 39, 46
Toys 49
Tractor 43
Trade 16
Traffic lights were first used in the USA in 1918.
Tram 58, 59, **63**
Transformer 29
Transistor 31, 83
Transplant surgery 55, 89
Transport 57
Treadmill crane 24

▲ Transistor, 1948

Trevithick, Richard (1771–1833) English engineer 58
Triode radio valves were invented by Lee de Forest, USA, in 1906.
Trousers 48
Tull, Jethro (1674–1741) English farmer and inventor 43
Tunnel 38, **39**
Turbine 28
Typewriter 77, **77**
Tyre 61

U
Umbrella 46
Underground railroad 62

▼ Telephone, 1876

Universal joint. Designed by Robert Hooke in 1675, the universal joint has been used ever since to change the direction of a force.

V
Vaccination 52, 54
Vacuum cleaner 46, **47**
Vacuum flasks were invented by Sir James Dewar (GB) in 1892.
Vesalius, Andreas (1514–64) Belgian anatomist 52, **54**
Videotape 90
Violin 84
Virus 54
Volta, Alessandro (1745–1827) Italian physicist 29

▲ Wheel, 3000 BC

W
Wallpaper 39

Wankel engine 59, 61
Warfare 69–73
Washing machine 46, **47**
Water clock 79, **79**
Water closet 47
Watermill 24
Water supply 35, 39; aqueduct **35**, 37; drains 46
Water wheel 21, 24, 27
Watt, James (1736–1819) Scottish engineer 27
Weapons 9, 12, 68–73
Wedge 20
Well 20, 25
Wheel 13, **13**, 57, **58**
Wheelbarrow 35, **36**
Winch 35
Windlass 20
Windmill 21, **21**, 24
Woodcut 80, **80**
Wright, Orville (1871–1948) and Wilbur (1867–1912) US pioneers of manned flight 66, **67**
Writing 74, 76

X, Z
X-rays 55
Zip fastener 48, **48**
Zeppelin, Count Ferdinand von (1838–1917) German airship designer 66, **67**
Zworykyn, Vladimir (born 1889) 86

ACKNOWLEDGEMENTS

Picture Research: Penny Warn

Photographs: Endpapers Cycles Peugeot; Page 4/5 Laserium, the cosmic laser concert created by Laser Images Inc., California. At the London Planetarium; 6 Metropolitan Museum of Art, New York *left*, Zefa *top right*, Dearborn Steel Works *bottom right*; 8 Michael Holford; 13 British Museum; 14 Metropolitan Museum of Art, New York; 16 Peter Clayton *top*, British Museum *center*, 17 Whitefriars Glassworks; 18 Sonia Halliday; 20 Giraudon; 21 Michael Holford *bottom*, Ronan Picture Library *top left*, Sonia Halliday *right*; 22 Zefa; 24 Zefa; 25 Zefa *top*; 28 Mansell; 29 Atomic Energy Authority *left*, Mobil *right*; 30 Derby Museum and Art Gallery *top left*, British Industrial Plastics Ltd. *bottom*; 30/31 Mansell; 31 Datsun Inc. *top right*, Dearborn Steel Works *bottom*; 40 Fitzwilliam Museum; 44 Chicago Historical Society; 46 Mansell *top*, *center*, 48 Aero Zip *top*, Peter Clayton *center*, 49 Peter Clayton *top right*, British Museum *center*, Mary Evans Picture Library *bottom*; 50 Australia News & Information Service; 52 Mary Evans Picture Library *left*; 54 Rijksmuseum *top left*, Mansell *top right*, *center*; 55 Mansell *bottom*; 56 Zefa; 63 Science Museum *top*, Louisville & National Railway *left*, Bildarchiv Preussischer Kulturbesitz *right*; 66 Mary Evans Picture Library *top left*, Mansell *top right*, British Aircraft *bottom*; 67 Science Museum *top left*, Mansell *top right*, Bell Aerospace Textron, Buffalo, N.Y. *center*, NASA *bottom*; 68 Victoria & Albert Museum; 70 British Museum *top*, *bottom*, Wallace Collection *center*; 72 Controller of HMSO *left*, Atomic Energy Authority *right*; 74 Giraudon; 76 Peter Clayton *top*; Royal Institute for the Blind *centre*, Sonia Halliday *bottom*; 76/77 British Museum; 77 Zefa; 78 Scala; 79 Mansell; 80 British Museum *left*; 82 Mary Evans Picture Library; 83 Mansell *top* Zefa *bottom*; 84 Zefa *top*, Italian Tourist Office *bottom*; 85 Edison National Historic Site *top*, Decca Record Co. *bottom*; 86 Science Museum; 87 Science Museum; 90 Musee d'Art et Histoire, Newchatel. Cover: Zefa *top*, *bottom left*, Science Museum *top right*; Zefa *back*.
Cover design by The Tudor Art Agency.